a Day at a Time

A THOUGHT AND A PRAYER FOR EACH DAY OF THE YEAR

DENIS DUNCAN

John Hunt
Publishing Limited

This reissue copyright © 2003 John Hunt Publishing Ltd

46A West Street, Alresford, Hants SO24 9AU, U.K.

Tel: +44 (0) 1962 736880 Fax: +44 (0) 1962 736881

E-mail: office@johnhunt-publishing.com

www.johnhunt-publishing.com

Text: © 1987 Denis Duncan

Design: Nautilus Design (UK)

ISBN 1 84298 118 8

A CIP catalogue record for this book is available from the British Library.

Printed in England by Ashford Colour Press Ltd Gosport, Hants

Contents

PREFACE

I offer 'a thought and a prayer' for each day of a year in the continuing hope that they will provide encouragement, strength and healing to those who receive them.

If readers happen to purchase this book mid-year, then just begin on that date and go on from there!

In the prayers I have, after consideration, decided to use 'You' rather than 'Thee'. I know some would prefer the more traditional form, but I feel the form chosen 'fits' the ethos of these particular prayers.

If, incidentally, an acknowledgement has not been made – for over periods of time one gathers material for use in preaching, lecturing and speaking without always recording the source at that moment – I would be glad to hear of the omission and will take the first opportunity available to repair it.

The only reason for offering a book of this kind is the possibility that it may help someone, somewhere, who needs to cope a little better. If that is achieved, its purpose has been met. I am glad the opportunity to publish *A Day at a Time* in one volume has arisen.

July 1987   DENIS DUNCAN

Preface to the second edition

It is a pleasure to have this book of "thoughts and prayers for a year" appear in a new format and I am grateful to John Hunt Publishing for making this possible. I have made no substantial alteration to the text, but attended only to references that needed updating.

May the reissue of *A Day at a Time* further extend the notable ministry the book has effected down the years!

October 2003   DENIS DUNCAN

JANUARY

Love Divine

January 1

A Thought

Love is the heartbeat of God. This is the message that comes from Jesus' actions and also, magnificently, from Paul's Hymn of Love (1 Corinthians 13). It is, moreover, the foundation and essence of The Golden Rule.

But why should we be surprised?

God *is* Love (1 John 4:8).

A Prayer
Let my love be sincere
  Help me
    to abhor that which is evil
      to cleave to that which is good
        to let the grace of God hold sway in my heart
Then shall I reflect Love Divine
  Through Jesus Christ, our Lord

Amen

January 2

A Thought

'Love Divine, all loves excelling' is the Love made manifest in Christ. There is only one way to deal with evil and it is for ever emblazoned on the scenario of *life*. It is the way of Love. Calvary was not something our Lord bore with reluctance or endured with bitterness. He saw death becoming victory. He knew Golgotha led to the Resurrection Garden.

Love conquered all.

A Prayer
If bitterness creeps into me

redeem it, O Lord
If envy dominates me
  redeem it, O Lord
If jealousy affects me
  redeem it, O Lord
If anger provokes me
  redeem it, O Lord
Then shall my human failings be turned to triumphs

Amen

January 3

A Thought
Love, in Jesus, accepted a three-fold denial, betrayal worth thirty pieces of silver and the insensitive cruelty expressed in crucifixion by people who did not know what they did.
Love so amazing, so divine...

A Prayer
You say, O Lord, that
  You will be betrayed
    Lord, is it I?
You say, O Lord, that
  You will be denied
    Lord, is it I?
Let me not crucify You afresh, O Lord
  putting You to an open shame
Let me rather glorify You
  in all I do

Amen

January 4

A Thought
Love Divine, incarnate, was seen in a man of courage, both physical and spiritual, who, in the hour of His ultimate

suffering, could cry: 'Father forgive them; for they know not what they do' (Luke 23:34).

　There was nothing Love did not face.

A Prayer
I lift up mine eyes to the hills
　and glory in Your name
I take my walk by the still waters
　and praise You for Your creation
1 walk in the valley of shadows
　and I feel Your strength
Thanks be to You, O God

　　　　　　　　　　Amen

January 5

A Thought
No matter how often we fail, or how awful our failure, the Divine Forgiveness is at hand. Love Divine can (as William Barclay translates it) 'stand any kind of treatment' for 'Love's first instinct is to believe in people.'

　'Love never regards anyone or anything as hopeless.'

A Prayer
Kindle within me, O Lord
　Zeal for service
　　enthusiasm for life
　　　admiration for good
Then my soul will glow
　with warmth and love

　　　　　　　　　　Amen

January 6

A Thought
Love does not dominate: it cultivates. It does not smother. It

offers a gift – to be accepted or declined.

It recognises the freedom of another to stay – or to go. Jesus did not hold back the rich young ruler when he decided, sadly, *he* could not stay.

Love will not override our individuality. That is not the way of God – who *is* Love.

A Prayer
Let Love dominate my hours but never people
Let Love cultivate all that is of beauty and holiness in others
    and in me too
So may our ways be
    ways of pleasantness
And all our paths
    be peace

                              Amen

January 7

A Thought
The Divine Kindness, desiring our good, will never stampede us into the Kingdom. Respecting our rights as personalities, it will rather lead us, gently, to the living water.

The Divine Patience waits and waits and waits, knowing that, drawn with the cords of Love, the prodigal will return.

A Prayer
When a new day dawns and life is a burden
    lift up my heart, O Lord
When the night comes and life is dark
    lift up my heart, O Lord
When the dawn breaks and all feels new
    Be lifted up in my heart, O Lord

                              Amen

January 8

A Thought
The Divine Love is of a kind that goes to ultimate lengths in its longing, waiting forgiveness. Such self-giving Love implies cost and pain. 'God so loved the world that He gave ...'

The Cross is the symbol of patient, long-suffering Love.

A Prayer
I wait on You, O Lord
  Speak, for I am ready to hear
I wait on You, O Lord
  Instruct, for I am ready to learn
I wait on You, O Lord
  Command, for I am ready to act
  Send me forth in Your name
  to serve You as You deserve
in obedience and with commitment
                              Amen

January 9

A Thought
The primacy of Love is written into the very fabric of 'life in the Spirit.' Loving relationships characterise all that life means. Between myself and God, there is a mystic union to be discovered – on God's initiative – just as there is between God and my neighbour. But if there is no 'horizontal' relationship between my neighbour and me which the 'vertical' relationship between myself and God makes essential, that mystical union becomes impossible.

It is no accident that the primacy of Love is expressed in the symbol of the Cross, where 'horizontal' and 'vertical' meet.

A Prayer
Teach me, O Lord
  the way of the Cross

the way of sacrifice
the way of obedience
the way of discipline
And so make my tiny crises
the way to resurrection and to life

Amen

January 10

A Thought
The life, death and resurrection of Jesus is a demonstration in history of God's refusal to 'think evil' of the world which despises and rejects Him. Let us not then 'think evil' of anyone if we would make our pattern that of the God of Love.

A Prayer
I lift up my hands in prayer, O Lord
and ask for blessing on them
I lift up my heart in prayer, O Lord
and ask for Love in it
I hold myself up before You, O Lord
and ask Your benediction

Amen

January 11

A Thought
God finds pleasure in the truth. Christ *is* the truth (John 14:6). The Holy Spirit *is* truth (1 John 5:6). But it is only when the Holy Spirit probes and penetrates our minds, our hearts and our 'unconscious' and brings about the fundamental change that will be expressed in new, patterns of action and reaction that we shall find gladness in the truth and never in others' misfortunes, sins or failures.

Love does not rejoice in iniquity but only in the truth (1 Corinthians 13:6).

A Prayer
Out of the depths
* I cry, O Lord*
Take me from the darkness
Lift my despair
Set my feet on new ground
And give me hope

Amen

January 12

A Thought

Hope is our salvation, for it lifts our eyes from the immediate and the material to a perspective divinely conditioned. From that perspective, Love 'hopeth all things.'

Neither Love Divine nor its human counterpart, can ever regard anyone or anything as hope-less.

A Prayer
When other helpers fail
* abide with me, O God*
When other comforts flee
* abide with me, O God*
Shine through the gloom
* and help me*
* triumph still*
O God, abide with me

Amen

January 13

A Thought

'It was man, not God, who needed to be reconciled' says William Barclay. 'Nothing had lessened the love of God: nothing turned that love to hate; nothing had ever banished that yearning from the heart of God. Man might sin, but God still loved.'

A Prayer
I hate the sins that make You grieve, O Lord
Grant that, out of my loathing of wrong
  there may come an embracing of good
Then may 1 see You, not grieving
  but glad because I am new

                    Amen

January 14

A Thought

'Nothing can happen that can break love's spirit. Love lasts for ever.' So runs part of 1 Corinthians 13 in the William Barclay translation.

It is important to hold on to words like these when the capacity to love is near breaking point.

As Thomas Hardy says: 'Love lures life on.'

A Prayer
Though all things are against me, O God
I know that nothing can separate me
  from Your love in Jesus Christ
May all things therefore be seen
  to be working together for good for me
    so long as 1 love You

                    Amen

January 15

A Thought

It is not the way of Divine Love to give humanity up, for Love holds to its 'first instinct' which is to believe in people. So our human love, patterned on the Divine Love must work and pray on the premise that there is the possibility of good in every one. Love is *never* without hope.

A Prayer
When the road is rough and my heart is weary
 give me of Your strength, O Lord
When the night is long and my fears build up
 give me of Your peace, O Lord
When the way is lonely and I feel bereft
 give me Your presence, O Lord
                    Amen

January 16

A Thought
Jesus, faced by His accusers, 'answered them nothing.' He did not need to, for nothing that they said really touched Him at all. He could maintain the silence of dignity.

   Love is not easily provoked! And Love was the very nature of the Christ whose inner strength enabled Him to face His accusers in dignified silence.

A Prayer
Bless me, Lord
  as I work
   as I play
    as l talk
     as I pray
So that through all I do, I may glorify Your name and bless people

                    Amen

January 17

A Thought
'Even a loving God is really not God because He loves,'
wrote P. T. Forsyth in *The Cruciality of the Cross*, 'but because He has power to subdue all things to the holiness of His Love as redeeming grace.'

A Prayer
As I reflect on the day that is past
 help me to
   recognise my failures and
   learn from them
So may I find something to pass on to others
 that will bless them on the way

Amen

January 18

A Thought

Our being called to love God *and* our neighbour is based and founded on the Divine Love 'which never faileth.' Though heaven and earth should pass away, that Love which is of God, 'lasts for ever.'

Our constant prayer must be for the gift of more of that unfailing Love within us, for it is unfailing love we are to offer in His name.

A Prayer
Grant me of the Love
 that never fails
So that, faced by the despair and misery of others
 I shall continue to help them
   at all times

Amen

January 19

A Thought

There is no way to defeat evil that excludes the facing of it. We cannot deny evil, avoid evil, rationalise evil or explain evil away. The only way to the glory of the resurrection is through the acceptance of death.

Christ reached the Garden of the Resurrection only after He had journeyed to the 'spirits in prison' by descending into hell. It is the only way, for it is an essential part of the redemptive healing process.

A Prayer
The day You gave, O Lord, is ended
For the constancy of Your comfort
  the consistency of Your love
    the company of Your presence
I give You thanks
You have never left me
  nor forsaken me, Lord
Journey with me still, I pray

Amen

January 20

A Thought

To walk the way of Love demands faith. To keep on walking the way of Love, whatever happens, demands hope. So faith and hope are the components without which we can never grow in Love.

These three stand together... the greatest being Love.

A Prayer
I mourn, O God
  wasted opportunities of
    learning
      teaching
        giving
But let me not worry over the time I have lost
Enable me rather to use the time that I have
  to serve You now

Amen

January 21

A Thought

The strength of gentleness! What a glorious translation – it is William Barclay's – of the word usually used, namely 'meek'. How accurately it fits our picture of God – the gentleness of the Shepherd and the strength of the Divine power. Somehow this phrase holds together – they must be together – the holiness and the Love of God in divine juxtaposition.

Blessed are the gentle who have inner strength.

Blessed are the strong who have the capacity to be gentle.

A Prayer
May the garments of humility my vesture be
So that I praise and glorify
   not myself
      but my Lord
Who offered Himself humbly for us all
Grant me then to be clothed
   in true humility

                              Amen

January 22

A Thought

You do not find the secret of magic by analysing its components. You do not explain falling in love simply by setting down certain psychological principles. The essence of both magic and falling in love is elusive but real.

'Love Divine, all loves excelling' is similarly not explained by an analysis of its elements. It is beyond human analysis in its scope *and* its depth.

Love is *of God*.

A Prayer
Let me drink freely
of the water of life, O Lord
Let me eat freely
of the bread of life, O Lord
So may I be nourished
unto life eternal

                   Amen

January 23

A Thought
'Pour in love where there is no love and you will draw love out.'
    So wrote St. John of the Cross, who understood Love Divine.

A Prayer
O God, it is a blessing
  that You understand
  for You have been there
    in the place of temptation
    in the place of pain
    in the valley of the shadows
    in loneliness and dereliction
Thanks be to You, O God
  for You know
    all that is in me
    all I have to face
    all my need
For Your Love Divine
  I humbly give You thanks

                   Amen

January 24

A Thought

Love is a serving that seeks no return, no thanks, no honour.
Love is the tireless touch that tells another: 'I am here.'
Love is the capacity to suffer with another, to give and to
retire un-noticed, ready only to answer the call again.

A Prayer
Give me the Love
  that will not seek its own
  that is not easily irritated
  that is not glad when things go wrong
For the best way of all is Love

                    Amen

January 25

A Thought

Love in the New Testament sense, must be proclaimed in its
wholeness by the people of God, 'the church'. It must be made
real in the body of Christ, 'the church'. It must be expressed in
the service of the community of grace, 'the church'.

'The church' must incarnate Love Divine.

A Prayer
Make my faith real, O God
  and so make me ready to risk
Make my hope real, O God
  and so make me ready to act
Make my love real, O God
  and so make me ready to serve
Make my peace real, O God
  and so make me ready to endure

                    Amen

January 26

A Thought

One of the saddest features of our times is the degradation of love in such phrases as 'making love' or 'having sex.' Love is not 'made', certainly not in a purely physical way. It is the fundamental attitude out of which all action comes and so embraces, not a part, but the whole. Love is of God (1 John 4:7). God is Love (4:8). The kind of love we have is an expression of the in-dwelling God within us (4:12). To prostitute this love into 'making love' is to damage the most fundamental concept of all. For human love must reflect Love Divine.

A Prayer
May I gaze at the heavens
  and praise You, O God
May I encounter the good and lovely
  and praise You, O God
May I feel the wonder of love
  and praise You, O God
May I know the Child of Bethlehem
  and praise You even more

Amen

January 27

A Thought

'Spare no effort to possess love.' So William Barclay renders the words 'Follow after charity' in 1 Corinthians 14:1 – immediately following the great hymn of Love. The *Jerusalem Bible* echoes that demand with its demand: 'You must want love more than anything else.' 'Put love first' says the *New English Bible*.

The development of love, though it is the gift of God, demands effort by us.

A Prayer
Capture my will, O God
  and make it free to serve You
Capture my heart, O God
  and fill it with love divine
Capture my enthusiasm, O God
  so that I may serve You as You desire

Amen

January 28

A Thought

Where Christianity is presented as an extreme, we must 'test the spirits' to see if they are of God. Wholeness is based on a true sense of balance.

Jesus was unique, but He was wholly balanced, and everything He said or did bears witness to His being just that. In this He was the perfect man.

A Prayer
O God
Let my ordered life be witness to Your presence within
Let my unwillingness to follow the crowd or go with the tide
  testify to the presence of Your Spirit
Let my balance be a reflection of Your peace within
Let my vision show that I have been with Jesus

Amen

January 29

A Thought

There is personal evil, as we all know – for it is our experience. There is evil in the world we know – for it is also our experience. But there is evil too in the cosmos itself. St Paul talks rightly of the 'rulers of the darkness of this world', which are not flesh and blood, but are principalities and powers –

spiritual wickedness in high places.

This does not however need to disturb us. Christ is Lord of Creation as well as Lord of our lives. Love Divine *is* over all.

A Prayer
Let me not fear
  the evil that is around me or
  the evil that is within me
    for You are greater than evil
    You transform it into good
I bless You Lord for You are the
  Redeemer of Life

Amen

January 30

A Thought
  A word from Thomas a Kempis' *The Imitation of Christ*:
  'Love is watchful
    and sleeping, slumbereth not
  Though weary,
    it is not tired
  Though pressed,
    it is not straitened
  Though alarmed,
    it is not confounded
  But, as a lively and burning torch,
    it forces its way upwards
    and securely passes through all.'

A Prayer
Let my love grow richer, Lord
Let my heart be full
Let my Faith grow stronger, Lord
Let my mind be cool

Let my Peace grow deeper, Lord
Becoming an unfathomable pool

                                        Amen

January 31

A Thought
   'May the day break
      the shadows flee away
   And Love be waiting for you
      at the end of every day'

A Prayer
Lord, bless this day
   May each hour be fruitful
   each minute creative
   each second valuable
At eventide
   may I rest in peace
      fulfilled
         serene
            receptive
   ready for tomorrow's tasks
Through Jesus Christ, our Lord

                                        Amen

FEBRUARY

The Loving Way

February 1

A Thought

'Holiness,' said Henry Drummond, in *The Greatest Thing in the World*, 'is in infinite compassion for others. Greatness is to take the common things of life and walk truly among them. Happiness is a great love and much serving.'

A Prayer
There is so much, O God
  I do not know
There is so much
  I have not done
But there is still that which
  I can learn and can do
Give me the energy and enthusiasm
  both to learn and to do
    what is Your will
Through Jesus Christ, our Lord

                    Amen

February 2

A Thought

It is clear from the 'golden rule' quoted by Jesus (Luke 10:27) that Love is about relationship. Love is to be expressed in that 'eternal triangle' made up of God, my neighbour and me.

There is a breakdown in Love if one side of the triangle drops out – for example 'if a man says "I love God" while hating his brother, he is a liar' (1 John 4:20).

The broken relationship with a brother denies the existence of a relationship of Love to God.

...ered Cross, O God

division in the church
division in the home
division in the world
division in the sacrament
Bring together that which is broken
  and make our unity complete
  to reflect the One-ness that is Divine
  and is true relationship

Amen

February 3

A Thought
'Life in the Spirit' is both 'one to one' in relation to God and 'communal' in relation to life in the world. There is no distinction between 'individual' and 'social' religion, for the spiritual life holds both together, in true relationship.

If we seek mystical union without community involvement, we shall have only an empty piety. If we are socially conscious in such a way as to obliterate personal faith, we shall do good social work, but it will not be 'life in the Spirit.'

We are to love God *and* our neighbour, at all times.

A Prayer
Cleanse the deep, unknown places of my heart
So that the pressures that push me towards evil
  are turned into the compassion that compels me to do good
Turn my upside-down life the right way up
And make it both a song of praise
  and a medium of Your Love

Amen

February 4

A Thought

We must endeavour, with grace, to bear the unbearable, endure the
unendurable; be patient with those who try our patience, be kind to
those who make themselves intolerable; be loving to those whom we
find it hard to love; *always for Christ's sake.*

A Prayer
The day to come is full of hope
Thanks be Yours, O Lord
The day I begin is full of opportunity
  Grace be mine, O Lord
The day I end has been blessed
Joy be Yours and mine, O Lord

Amen

February 5

A Thought

Growth in love can come only through struggle and pain. Love is a
gift but the process of developing the gift and learning the full
meaning of what is offered, makes effort and struggle unavoidable.
'How can I love?' we sometimes ask almost in despair, for some are
not easy to love.

Jesus, in agony in the Garden of Gethsemane, 'prayed more
earnestly.'

So must we pray the more earnestly in the struggle to love.

A Prayer
Let me not be superficial
  in thought
    in word
      in deed

But grant me, in the deep places
  conviction
    consistency
      compassion
So that from my depths, I may
give to the deep needs of others

                              Amen

February 6

A Thought

A 'non-judgemental' attitude relates to acceptance of people in whatever situations they find themselves, *as a basis for working towards something better*. God accepts us as we are, but always in order to take us to where we ought to be!

A Prayer
In the spring of life
  give us joyous enthusiasm
In the summer of life
  grant us the satisfaction of true success
In the autumn of life
  help us to give of all we have learnt
In the winter of life
  enable us to grow older gracefully
Until the spring comes

                              Amen

February 7

A Thought

Although she *sinned* greatly – her sins were forgiven because she *loved* greatly.

I find this juxtaposition of great sin and great love in Jesus' words to Simon about the woman who 'drenched Jesus' feet with her tears' one of the most truly comforting sentences in the Bible.

A Prayer
Look on us, Lord, with compassion
  as we struggle with
    temptation
     tiredness
      truth
Assure us of Your forgiveness
  Add to our strength
   Illuminate our understanding
So that what feels like trial and tribulation may
  become opportunities for growth in grace

                           Amen

February 8

A Thought
'Peace,' says Sister Eva of Friedenshort, 'is "Love resting".'

A Prayer
For Love's sake I rush
to give
  to do
   to help
    to strengthen
Bless what I do in the name of Love
But
  to give
  I must receive
  to offer
  I must obtain
  to bring love
  I must have Love
  Grant me the peace of
  Love resting
so that my love may be renewed

                           Amen

February 9

A Thought
The 'giving out' of love demands effort and energy. There must then come a time when love must rest and 'take in'.

That is what Peace is. It is love resting – in order to be love renewed.

A Prayer
Let Love come down
  to enfold the world
    to redeem its life
      to enhance its future
Let Love come down
  to inspire hope
    to increase faith
      to deepen our love

                    Amen

February 10

A Thought
How necessary it is to rest! How difficult it can be to rest; especially to rest our minds. We can lay the body down and even fall asleep, yet the mind is not stilled. We sleep 'officially', but in dreams and nightmares our agitated souls make their sleepless presence felt in anxious tribulation.

The Peace of Love resting must be found. The tumult of the winds and waves of anxiety must be quickened by the One who eternally says: 'Peace, be still!'

For 'the winds ceased and there was a great calm.'

A Prayer
Lead me, O Lord
  to understand
    the broken heart
    the confused mind

the sensitive spirit
the desolate soul
And understanding more
Lead me, O Lord, through the influence of Your Spirit
to heal the troubled heart
to still the restless mind
to ease the pain of over-sensitivity
to strengthen the weary soul
And all to Your glory

Amen

February 11

A Thought

Peace, says the Psalmist, is the recovery of something lost. 'He gave me *back* my peace' (Psalm 55:18, *New English Bible*).

The heart cries out for relationship with God to be restored. The mind persistently pursues ways to reconciliation. The soul longs for the union fractured by our waywardness. The whole creation 'groans' (the Psalmist uses this word as well as Paul) to be at one with God. 'Our hearts are restless till they rest in Thee.'

But all is truly well.

He gives us back our Peace.

A Prayer
If my vision is poor
illumine the way for me, O God
If my enthusiasm is lagging
stimulate my soul, O God
If my mind is blurred
clarify my discernment, O God
If my life is wayward
make me new, O God
So may I receive back my purpose
and my peace

Amen

February 12

A Thought

'May the Lord of peace himself give you peace at all times, wherever you may be.'

This peace-full benediction comes from 2 Thessalonians 3:16 (*New English Bible* footnote).

A Prayer
Grant me, O Lord
  purity of heart
  a clean mind
  a body which is the temple
    for Your Spirit
  and a soul at peace
Thus, equipped
  may I meet through strength within
  whatever I have to face without

Amen

February 13

A Thought

The presence of the divine Love and Peace in our lives has profound practical consequences – for example an ability to cope with criticism and hostility and to stand up to pressure.

There was a time when Jesus had to stand before His accusers and listen to their impertinent and blasphemous questions with, as I have called it, 'the silence of dignity' (January 16). But 'He answered them nothing.'

That attitude is a model for us for, with peace and love, we can move towards similar personal strength.

A Prayer
Your Love bids me welcome and my soul does eat
For You are the bread life to me

Your Love bids me welcome and my soul does drink
For You are the living water to me
Blessed am I when I hunger and thirst after righteousness For I know
I shall be filled

Amen

February 14

A Thought

Kindness is inherent in the one-ness of mankind. All that destroys this kinship is diabolical and must force the Christian into the fight against racial intolerance and prejudice, the greed which produces 'haves' and 'have nots', the passions which create wars and rumours of war, the unconscious drives, individual and collective, that are expressed in sheer selfishness.

We cannot speak of kindness without committing ourselves wholly to the practical action that speaks of fellowship, of unity and of concern.

A Prayer
Let me not dabble in words that delay action
Let me not philosophise about love, but express it
Let me not theorise about grace, but show it
Let me not question risk, but take it

Amen

February 15

A Thought

Only the wounded surgeon can heal, said Carl Jung. So it is in all healing. Only the wounded healer can truly heal.

A Prayer
You were despised and rejected of men, O Lord
A man of sorrows and acquainted with grief
So You can understand when I feel rejected
You can I feel my sorrow and my sadness

I thank You for Your presence
  in all my times of darkness
  and for giving me Light along my way

                    Amen

February 16

A Thought
The service of the Kingdom is not effected by 'supersaints' but by ordinary people made extra-ordinary through the Spirit. They know the loving way, so show it.

A Prayer
O use me, Lord
  just as You will and when and where
Take such talents as I have
  and turn them to good for You
Take such weaknesses as I have
  and redeem them for use by You
Take my moments and my days
  let them flow in ceaseless praise
Take my life and let it be
  consecrated to You, O Lord

                    Amen

February 17

A Thought
'Who hath ears to hear, let him hear.' It is possible to hear officially but fail to 'hear' in the sense that a message really registers. It is possible to 'see' but not to 'notice' in the sense of 'taking note.'
To see and actually 'take note of', to hear and actually 'listen', are important aspects of caring.

Pay attention! It is part of the loving way!

A Prayer
Give me, O God, a sensitive and understanding attitude
   when the sad seek solace
      the despairing, hope
      the unlucky, sympathy
      the defeated, comfort
Grant me the grace to give of myself abundantly
Aware that You have given so much for me

                              Amen

February 18

A Thought

There are three degrees of pain that must move to compassion: the pain of the abysmally lonely; the pain of those overwhelmed with guilt; and the pain of those separated, not by geography but by circumstance, from those they love most.

   May there be 'balm in Gilead' for all of them.

A Prayer
When we walk through
   a vale of tears
      take our hands, O Lord
When we dance over
   a mountain of laughter
      clap Your hands, O Lord
When we stand in the
   valley of decision
      take our arm, O Lord
And let us know that, always
those everlasting arms are underneath

                              Amen

February 19

A Thought

'Phares begat Esrom' (Matthew 1:3). And there are many other 'begats' in that chapter!

It is worth stopping and thinking on that phrase for it is a reminder how unknown, unsung people played a part in the providential chain that gave us Christ.

We do not always know – or need to know – what we are contributing to the Kingdom.

A Prayer
When I am in sorrow
  comfort me, O Lord
When I am anxious
  stay with me, O Lord
When I am care-full and troubled about many things
  give me perspective, O Lord
Then will I take no anxious thought
  for yesterday, today or tomorrow
                    Amen

February 20

A Thought

There can hardly be a more moving book than Maude Royden's *A Three-Fold Cord*. It tells of the life-long relationship of profound love between Dr. Hudson Shaw and herself, lived out so successfully in the Shaws' house. Dr Royden writes:

The day came when Hudson's doctor told me he would not live more than twenty-four hours. I sat beside him, counting the moments, but now I didn't try to call him back. He wanted to live, but the struggle was too great. That mortal fatigue which had possessed him often when in the height of his powers was no longer to be denied. I could not wish him to endure it longer.

He fell into unconsciousness and in his sleep he died. He had no pain and I was with him, his hand in mine.

We had forty-three years of work and love and we had been married eight weeks and three days.

For all this I thank God.

A Prayer
My times are in Thy hand, O Lord
 may I thank You for all the time I have
 may I use the time given me
 may I redeem whatever time I lose, through failure
 may I make my time a time of blessing, for all
      Amen

February 21

A Thought

There is, sometimes, a harshness of judgement and attitude in 'the church' towards those who wrestle with temptation. This should not be, for it does not represent the God we know in Jesus Christ. Those who are called to pastoral ministry must always hear within themselves that awe-inspiring phrase: 'There but for the grace of God, go I.'

If, indeed, they have gone through the fire themselves, let them count it a privilege, for under the grace of God, they will have learned the full meaning of the attribute of empathy and its part in the redemption of people.

A Prayer
May I always
 in heavenly love
  abide
So may I find
 security
  strength
   peace
    serenity

      Amen

February 22

A Thought

When Jesus set a child 'in the midst', I wonder if He was trying to tell us about holy innocence, the sense of wonder and the joy of a simple faith.

I am sure the Kingdom of God is 'of such.'

A Prayer
Make me, O Lord
  an instrument of peace
  a tool for service
  a means of grace
Refine me, O Lord, in such a way
  that my best may be of use
  that my worst may be redeemed for service
  that my strengths may be humbly offered
  that my weaknesses may be made strong
So may grace bring much to me from You
And I, through grace, bring much to others
  in Your name

Amen

February 23

A Thought

Kindness is never possessiveness, nor is it manipulation. It is an offering in love of that which we can give, in the hope that if the gift is accepted, someone will be blessed.

A Prayer
Accept, O God
  the gifts I offer
    in return for all Your Love imparts to me
Accept too
  that which You most desire
    the gift of my humble, thankful heart

Amen

February 24

A Thought

It must have been very difficult for Jesus to speak to Martha as strongly as He did for He 'loved Martha' (John 11:5). I wonder if the strength of His statement to her was a response not to that one incident, but to Martha's usual reaction to spiritual matters? It is in that area that the leap of faith, the operation of intuition and the ability to accept the possibility of 'Divine surprises' is so necessary, but is this where Martha fell short of expectation?

Jesus' words were, I suspect, an essential ministry to Martha, and part of His loving way.

A Prayer
Help me, O God, to make
  right choices
    right decisions
      right relationships
Let me be objective in my judgements
  while keeping in touch with Your voice within
So may I forward that which is right

                    Amen

February 25

A Thought

How prominent hands are in the Bible! Moses upheld hands meant victory. The healing hands of Christ were available to the sick. Hands of blessing were laid on the children. The disciples were set apart by 'laying on of hands'. Then to sum it all up – there are praying hands, of course, the hands that together point to God.

A Prayer
Take my hands, O Lord
  'Let them move
    at the impulse of Thy love'

Take my feet, O Lord
  'Let them be swift and beautiful
    for Thee'
Take myself, O Lord
  'I shall be
    ever
      only
        all
          for Thee'

                    Amen

February 26

A Thought

'It is terrible,' says Yevtushenko, the Russian poet, 'to replace dead feelings with memories of feelings.'

  How true!

A Prayer
Thanks be to You, O Lord
  for love divine, all loves excelling
  for love divine, made known through human love
Make us who receive love
  givers of love to others and so
  givers of Love to You
Accept our love, which is possible because
  You first loved us

                    Amen

February 27

A Thought

Envy must be recognised and resisted in every area of life. In personal life it can sour relationships, stir up feelings, sabotage sanctification and stunt the growth of Christian Love. Unchecked, uncontrolled, unaccepted, unredeemed, it can destroy inner growth, inner peace, inner strength and inner security.

It is a deadly sin, indeed, and never part of the loving way.

A Prayer
Let me harbour no evil thoughts, O Lord
 the thoughts of the lower nature
 the thoughts of the envious heart
 the thoughts of the unredeemed mind
Let Your Spirit flow into my being
 to transform me and make me new
 a new creation in Christ

Amen

February 28

A Thought
The slogan of the Salvation Army is 'Christ for the world, the world for Christ.' The Salvation Army Goodwill Centre in Amsterdam adds: 'The Gospel in Word *and Deed.*'

A Prayer
I ask, O God
 give me
I seek, O God
 help me find
I knock, O God
 open to me
So may I learn the riches
 of Your grace
Through Jesus Christ, our Lord

Amen

February 29 (Leap Year)

A Thought
Those who have *Mary* among their names must feel greatly blessed for

it seems, from the Gospel story, that those with the closest relationships with Christ were Marys. There was *Mary, Jesus' mother,* who noted all He said and did. She 'kept these things and pondered them in her heart.'

There was *Mary of Bethany* who chose the 'one thing needful', the part that was 'best' and 'would not be taken away.'

There was *Mary Magdalene* to whom Jesus, on the resurrection morn, said *Mary* and made her *look in the right direction.*

A *Mary* at His birth.

A *Mary* by his cross... indeed three Marys (John 19:25).

A *Mary* at His resurrection

No wonder the angel said to *Mary* (Luke 1:28).

'You are the most blessed of women.'

A Prayer
Thanks be to You, O God
  for the gifts of women
  for the gentle graces of femininity
  for the graceful gentleness of Your handmaid
Thanks be to You for the ministry of women in Your Son's
  life, death and resurrection
Through Jesus Christ, our Lord

Amen

MARCH

Come, let us worship...

March 1

A Thought

T. S. Eliot's words on the wall at Little Gidding, Huntingdon, Cambridgeshire, England remind us of the purpose of worship. It is a time not for argument, but for awareness of the Love Divine that excels all loves.

'You are not here to verify,
Instruct yourself or inform curiosity
Or carry report
You are here to kneel
where prayer has been valid.'

A Prayer
I feel Your presence near, Lord
  in my quiet walking
  in my silent reading
  in my meditation
Let my heart be Your home
  Live in me
    I pray
Through Jesus Christ, our Lord

                                    Amen

March 2

A Thought

'They come, the tired travellers, to find green herbs and ample bread, quiet and brother's love and humbleness, Christ's peace on every head.'

These words of invitation and experience were written of Monte Cassino, St. Benedict's own monastery. To arrive there must in itself have been an experience of grace abounding.

A Prayer
Faint and weary
  I wait on You, O Lord
    and so recover the strength
      to run and not be weary
        to walk and not faint
With strength renewed
  let me mount up on eagle's wings
  and feel the resurrection joy

                    Amen

March 3

A Thought

The disciples on the road to Emmaus discussed the life, death and resurrection of the Christ, the Messianic hopes associated with Him and the phenomena rumoured to be taking place in Jerusalem. Yet they were unaware of His presence.

Is this not a cautionary tale?

We can talk religion and discuss theology but still be insensitive to the presence of 'the Christ in the midst' even as we do it. Equally we can go through the externals of worship and never 'draw nigh to God.'

It is worth remembering that, for the good of our souls.

A Prayer
Where distance divides
  O Lord, be near
If separation comes
  O Lord, go not away
Across the distance of necessity or circumstance
  cast Your enfolding Love
so that spiritual nearness may bless us
  when the hurt of distance brings its pain

                    Amen

March 4

A Thought

J. S. Whale once commented that we find it easier to 'run round the burning bush, taking photographs from various angles, instead of taking off our shoes from our feet, because the place whereon we tread is holy ground.'

A Prayer
Looking unto Jesus
   may I see
      the Way
        the Truth
         the Life
And still looking, find through Him
   fulfilment
      joy
        and peace

                 Amen

March 5

A Thought

No one looks for loneliness, but we must all search for solitude. Without our personal 'desert', we miss the riches offered to us through the Holy Spirit.

A Prayer
I come to You, O God
   in the silence
      to know myself
      to meet with You
Praise be to You for the opportunity
   of the encounter
   that leads to life

                 Amen

March 6

A Thought

William Temple, the great Archbishop of Canterbury, said that, while he was aware many strange happenings credited to prayers are no more than coincidences, he could not help noticing that when he did not pray, meaningful coincidences just did not seem to happen.

A Prayer
Lord, may I see Your hand
  in the timing of the rainbow
  in coincidence and happening
  in the joy of surprise encounter
  in the mystery of miracle
And so rejoice greatly

Amen

March 7

A Thought

Soren Kierkegaard came to think of prayer as man's greatest earthly happiness, so it is not surprising that this great Dane (in truth!) speaks so profoundly on the subject. You ought not to ask for reasons for praying, he says. Praying is like breathing: if you don't breathe, you die. So, if you don't pray, you die spiritually.

A Prayer
I pray to You, O God
  in need
    in love
      in obedience
Answer, O Lord
  not in proportion to my faith
    but in the wonder of Your Love
So will I be truly blessed

Amen

March 8

A Thought
The Church is Christ's body, having one faith, serving one Lord, scattered (like salt) in the world to create a climate of grace (the salt must not lose its savour) and taking on the responsibility to make humanity aware that life abundant, true life that is, takes on the spiritual dimension without which no one can be in their true element.

A Prayer
I believe in You, O God
  You are the source of my life
I believe in You, O Christ
  You are the Son of the living God
I believe in You, O Holy Spirit
  You are energy divine
Confirm my belief and establish my faith, I pray

Amen

March 9

A Thought
This parable comes from *Challenge and Response*:
One spring the fleet-winged mallard built her nest upon an old stone bridge over a quiet moat. To each tiny duckling it must have seemed a hazardous drop from the warm protection of the nest down to the sparkling water twelve feet below. Yet when they were only two days old, their mother flew down on to the moat and called them: called them out of all that seemed so necessary and familiar and secure into a strange world. And they obeyed, coming three at a time, each little group waiting for their call, then venturing their lives into the unknown... to find themselves in their true element.

A Prayer
Grant us, O Lord
  Patience and self-control when we are misunderstood
  The honesty to acknowledge when we misunderstand
  The insight to realise our hidden motives
  The grace that will redeem our self-centred ways
And help us be in our true element

Amen

March 10

A Thought
The Church is people, people called together to be the people of God, and with the responsibilities such a calling involves. The vindication of that election, that 'chosen-ness', is always demonstrated in humility and never in self-righteousness or spiritual arrogance.

Election to service is a humbling privilege.

A Prayer
May I give thanks for everything
May I learn through whatever I experience
May I use every opportunity to find the way and the truth
So may my time be redeemed
  and my days enhanced

Amen

March 11

A Thought
All 'the means of grace' in Christian practice and tradition relate to the concept of growth towards a more mature Christian life marked by progressive change in the balance between 'flesh' and 'spirit', 'temporal' and 'eternal', self-righteousness and humility.
Prayer, worship, the sacraments, fellowship will all help to keep us 'in balance.'

A Prayer
Your mercies, O Lord, are
  new every morning
Your forgiveness, O Lord, is
  real every day
Your presence, O Lord, is
  there every night
Your Love, O Lord, is
  always around me
May I live with the joy of that knowledge

Amen

March 12

A Thought
The Sacrament of the Lord's Supper, Communion Service, Eucharist or Mass – however you see this act of worship in your own branch of the church is a supreme example of profound simplicity. It is simple in that it is an action sermon that speaks for itself, but it goes, at the same time, into profound depths – of our own need *and* of God's love. Never let us abuse, devalue or trivialise the Sacrament.

A Prayer
Help me, O God
  to be true to myself
    in everything I proclaim
    in all I offer in any service I render
If this costs me friends, position, popularity, affection
  Prevent me from bitterness, self-pity and apathy
  Prevail on me to be more loving and understanding
  Provide me with the strength and inner peace to speak
  the truth in love

Amen

March 13

A Thought
To be within sight and sound of the Sacrament of the Lord's Supper is to experience the climate of grace. As the centurion at the Cross was forced to proclaim some kind of divinity emanating from the crucified prophet he did not know, so the heart will cry out in the Sacrament that the divine presence is truly 'in the midst.'

'The bread and wine remove,
  but Thou art here
Nearer than ever...'

A Prayer
When my mind is clouded by depression
When my heart is overwhelmed with anxiety
When my soul is heavy with guilt
  Be my Vision
    my Comforter
      my Saviour
Then shall I know peace again

                    Amen

March 14

A Thought
Pentecost is concerned with *both* personal responsibility (the tongues of fire settled on *each one* of the disciples) *and* community growth ('they were all with one accord in one place.')

The community of grace is composed of individuals receptive to and accepting grace in fellowship.

A Prayer
When all is against us
  circumstances or people

Help us
to look and learn
to love and give
And so turn what seems to be bad
into good

Amen

March 15

A Thought
There are various factors at work in 'close encounters' with the divine. I am sure they include direct communion (as in Isaiah 6), synchronicity (Moses and the burning bush), symbol (as in the story of the road to Emmaus) and relationship (when 'the gardener' said 'Mary', Mary said 'Master'.)

A Prayer
You are the Author of my faith
for any growth begins in Your grace
You are the Finisher of my faith
for I am complete only in You
'Finish then Thy new creation
Pure and spotless let it be'

Amen

March 16

A Thought
The 'annihilation of selfhood' is part of the mystic way, says F. C. Happold in *Mysticism*. 'He who would tread the Mystic Way is bidden not only painfully to learn to annihilate the selfhood but also to turn his attention more and more from the multiplicity of the phenomenal world, with its classifying and image-making, its logical reasoning and discursive thinking, so as to attain that 'single seeing' of

which the mystics speak; for not until the eye has become wholly single can the whole body become full of light.'

A Prayer
O God
   Let mine eye be single
    and my body full of light
   Keep me looking unto Jesus
    the Light of the World
   So may my light shine in the darkness
    and others find light along their way, too

                  Amen

March 17

A Thought
True ecstasies *amplify* the intelligence and the will instead of depressing them, and especially instead of annihilating them.

   This guideline by Poulain, the French authority on mysticism, is a warning *and* an encouragement to all on the spiritual path.

A Prayer
I bless You, O Lord, nor do I
   forget all Your benefits
   You do 'forgive iniquities'
    and have done so for me
   You do 'heal diseases'
    and have done so for me
   You do 'redeem Life'
    and make it new
   You do 'crown us with loving-kindness and tender mercy'
I bless You for this experience of Love

                  Amen

March 18

A Thought
Karl Rahner (in his book *Meditations on Freedom and the Spirit*) says this in talking about true freedom:

'A man can always let himself be so busy that he is rushed through the multifarious activities of his life... He can always forget himself in his concern with the thousand and one details he has to deal with... But he never will really become free of himself in this way. The totality, the oneness of his existence, which he is trying to push away and forget in his daily life, will always rise from the background gloom to which it has been consigned and constantly put before him and his freedom the ultimate question of how he relates to his totality and not just of the thousand details of his life.'

A Prayer
'Make me a captive Lord
And then I shall be free
Help me to render up my sword
And I shall conqueror be'
Grant us, O Lord
  Freedom in Christ
Knowing the truth
  May we truly feel free

Amen

March 19

A Thought
'Take no notice of that feeling you get of wanting to leave off in the middle of your prayer,' says St. Teresa, 'but praise the Lord for the desire you have to pray.'

A Prayer
I give You thanks, O Lord
  for bread

and birds
    and beasts
for grace
    and gifts
        and generosity
And for all that speaks of Your goodness
    Thanks be to You

Amen

March 20

A Thought

'I would like to make a plea for prayer as the creative way of being unavailable.' This startling request is made by Henri Nouwen in *The Living Reminder*. He goes on: 'A certain unavailability is essential for the spiritual life of the minister. How would it sound, when the question "Can I speak to the minister?" is not answered by "I am sorry, he has someone in his study" but by "I am sorry, he is praying"? When someone says "The minister is unavailable because this is his day of solitude, because this is his day in the hermitage, this is his desert day"? Could not that be a consoling ministry?'

A Prayer
Leave me not comfortless, O God
    come to me
Let not my heart be troubled
    nor let it be afraid
Leave Your peace with me
    the peace you give to us
I believe in You, O God
    and in Your Son, Jesus
So I know I am never alone

Amen

March 21

A Thought

We may only yet 'see through a glass darkly', not 'face to face.' We know only in part, not in whole. But a foretaste of the blessing that is to come is ours. We know what is to be is more glorious than we can conceive; is inexpressible in the vocabulary available to us in the here and now. We *are* 'touching and handling things unseen', 'sweet foretaste of the festal joy', indeed.

A Prayer
Grant me, O God
  the holy innocence of Mary
  the implicit trust of Joseph
  the simple faith of the shepherds
  the vision of the wise men
Then my worship will be real too

Amen

March 22

A Thought

There is not a single book in the Bible that does not mention the word 'peace'. If, moreover, you count up the number of times 'peace' is used, you approach three figures. It is no surprise then, that Jesus devotes one Beatitude to the sheer joy of peace-making.

Blessed indeed, are the makers of peace!

A Prayer
Take all that happens in life
  private and public
And work through it for our good
  and Your glory, O Lord
So we may see that through suffering and circumstances
You can make all things work together for good
  for those who serve You and love You

Amen

March 23

A Thought

Father Andrew's simple but profound prayer is a helpful way in which to begin a new day. He puts it this way:

Lord by Thy divine silence
  by Thy wondrous love
  by Thine adorable humility
Keep me quiet and still and
  possess me with Thy peace.

A Prayer
Assure me, O God, of Your Presence
Re-assure me, O God, of Your Forgiveness
Then shall I know the ever-present opportunity of renewal
And the joy of a new beginning

Amen

March 24

A Thought

Many people think of 'retreat' as escape, but nothing is further from the truth, for it is in retreat that we meet with the Reality that compels 'involvement' and determines its strength and quality.

It is 'involvement' without 'retreat' that is an irrelevance.

A Prayer
Bless me in solitude, O God
Bless me in community, O God for the gains of my solitude
can become my blessing on the community

Amen

March 25

A Thought

'You need hands,' Max Bygraves used to sing. We can add 'and fingers'. Together they symbolise individuality and corporateness. Each finger has some role. Together –including the thumb (try doing things without using it) – they do even more.

Just like the members of the church.

A Prayer
Help us, O Lord
  to use our skills
    to develop our talents
     to offer our gifts
Always for the good of people
  and the glory of Your name

                      Amen

March 26

A Thought

'To travel together, we must be sure of our destination' said the great Cardinal Suesens. It is an important statement about 'ecumenism' by a committed ecumenist. It is both encouraging – for there is much of the road we can travel together and it is cautionary – we cannot behave as if we had already arrived. The map should nevertheless be consulted together.

A Prayer
In the agony of decision
  strengthen me, O Lord
In the agony of loving
  understand me, O Lord
In the agony of temptation
  accept me, O Lord
In the agony of loneliness
  befriend me, O Lord

                      Amen

March 27

A Thought
John Taylor writes in *The Go-between God*: 'The beauty of holiness in the midst of this revolutionary world belongs to those who set the Lord always before their eyes.'

Let us 'worship the Lord in the beauty of holiness.'

A Prayer
When night comes
  let me sleep in peace, O Lord
When morning comes
  let me rise refreshed, O Lord
While today runs
  keep me enthusiastic, O Lord
When night returns
  may I feel fulfilled, O Lord

                    Amen

March 28

A Thought
We live in times of great emphasis on the need to be 'in touch with our feelings.' Douglas Meeks has a cautionary word on that in his Introduction to Jurgen Moltmann's *The Experiment Hope*. He writes: 'A theology that prizes experience higher than faith, will always shine brightly in its reflection of the times, but will soon fade with those times.'

A Prayer
'The Saviour comes!'
May I hearken to that glad sound, O God
  and welcome Him
So that my heart may 'exult with joy'
And my voice be filled with song

                    Amen

March 29

A Thought
As salt permeating the earth has its secret effect (Matthew 5:13), so must disciples influence the world. As light shining in the world so must disciples 'shine before men' (5:16).

Where salt is working and light shining, things will begin to happen. Life will begin to appear.

A Prayer
Walk with me, O Lord
  on my road to Emmaus
So that I may recognise
  Your presence
  And know You as Lord
And so 'constraining You'* to stay with me
  I shall be truly blessed

                    Amen
*Luke 24:29

March 30

A Thought
We can, of course, worship God on the hills or in the woods. May we often do so. But worship also means going from our sanctuaries to serve God in the world. Only then is worship complete and love fulfilled.

A Prayer
I pray for the world, O Lord, through
  that old refugee
    that hungry child
      that imprisoned writer
        that bereaved family

And as I pray I offer
  whatever I can do to reconcile
    anyone
      anywhere
Give me, I pray, the strength to do it
                    Amen

March 31

A Thought
The ass is, symbolically, the most stupid of animals, so it could not possibly stand comparison with sensible men. Nevertheless Balaam's ass saw the angel of the Lord (Numbers 22) while the prophetic man of God was totally blind to the spiritual presence; so blind that he cruelly and angrily denied 'the presence' by violently castigating the ass.

When we do not want to see the Lord, we go to extremes to ignore His presence. But He is there! 'Come, let us worship...'

A Prayer
Help me to see
  Wrong where there is wrong
    and repent
  Good where there is good
    and be glad
  Sincerity where there is integrity
    and be uplifted
  Freedom where You have made me free
    and be happy
Through Jesus Christ, our Lord
                    Amen

Easter Day

A Thought
'The Risen Christ comes to quicken a festival in the inner-most heart

of man. He is preparing for us a springtime of the Church: a Church devoid of means of power, ready to share with all, a place of visible communion for all humanity. He is going to give us enough imagination and courage to open up a way of reconciliation. He is going to prepare us to give our life so that man may no longer be victim of man.'

So ran the Easter Message, the 'joyful news,' from Taizé, the great international and ecumenical Community in France, when the decision to set up the 'Council of Youth' was announced to all. That Council was formed when 40,000 young people from 100 countries, gathered for this purpose. That Council has, since then, been 'a reality that gathers together youth from every land, committing us unambiguously on account of Christ and the Gospel . . . At the heart of the Council of Youth is the risen Christ.'

A Prayer
May Resurrection Joy
fill my whole being
body renewed
mind refreshed
heart filled
soul stilled
Turn every possibility of defeat into victory
every fear of default into triumph
every hint of doubt into certainty
every threat of weakness into life
Through Jesus Christ, our Lord

Amen

APRIL

Sharing and Caring

April 1

A Thought

'I will search for the lost, recover the straggler, bandage the hurt, strengthen the sick, leave the healthy and strong to play and give them their proper food.'

What remarkable words on loving pastoral care these are!* They come, of course, from Ezekiel (*New English Bible*, Ezekiel 34:15-16).

A Prayer
Forgive my 'foolish ways', O God
  and make me wise
If fool I must be,
  let it be only 'for Christ's sake'
And in such 'foolishness'
  may Yours be the glory
Through Jesus Christ, our Lord

                    Amen

* *These words are also quoted under November 21, but are included here again because of their special relevance to this month's theme.*

April 2

A Thought

To serve God is to serve mankind. In serving mankind we serve God.

  These two statements belong together.

A Prayer
Grant me the grace, O God
to forgive
  as I have been forgiven

to be merciful
*   for I have received mercy*
to love
as I have been loved
So may I fulfil the law of Christ

Amen

April 3

A Thought
Mother Julian, the Norwich mystic, had a cell with two windows, one opening into the church, through which she could receive communion, the other looking out into the garden. There, people came to receive her spiritual guidance.

The picture is a symbol of 'detachment' and 'participation' which together constitute discipleship.

A Prayer
Drop Thy still dews of quietness
*   Till all our strivings cease*
Take from our souls
*   the strain and stress*
And let our ordered lives confess
*   The beauty of Thy Peace*

Amen

(These words are by John Greenleaf Whittier)

April 4

A Thought
What could be nearer to the purpose of the coming of Christ than that a lonely, lost man should be accepted and treated as worth meeting? At last his true value is recognised. Zacchaeus is treated as a man of real stature, as one with whom the Son of Man could actually share a meeting.

A Prayer
Give me a grateful heart, O Lord
* for countless blessings*
*   innumerable opportunities*
*   infinite grace*
I thank You, O God
* for animals and birds*
*   girls and boys*
*   and all kinds of people*
I thank You, O God
* for Jesus Christ*
*   Saviour*
*   Redeemer*
*   Lord*
I thank You, O God

                                  Amen

April 5

A Thought

Jesus was severely criticised for associating with sinners, but the accusations did not really touch Him. He knew what He was doing and no superficial criticism affected His lovingness in any way.

If you are similarly accused, be at peace. So long as you know your motives and trust the Spirit moving within you, have no fear. God sees and knows your love. Leave it in His hands.

A Prayer
Give me, O God
* a sense of the height and depth*
*   of Your love*
Give me, too
* a sense of the length and breadth*
*   of Your love*
*   So may I offer the*

grandeur of that love
  to all who need it

                    Amen

April 6

A Thought

The development of the spiritual life and emphasis on the spiritual dimension is as important for balance in community health and growth as it is for individual welfare. It is this that brings the life of the Spirit into the practical life of the world.

An educational approach that ignores spiritual growth and development fails at the most crucial point. A political programme that takes no account of the essentially spiritual nature of man cannot ultimately minister to a people's good. A national health service that refuses to go beyond the bounds and limitations of orthodox medicine denies the reality of the other areas of man's nature.

Spiritual growth not only encourages more love to God: it generates so much more love to our neighbour.

A Prayer
I seek Your blessing, O God
  on all who struggle to survive
  on those who live in unreconciled family situations
  on all who are separated from those they love the most
  on those who faint and are weary

                    Amen

April 7

A Thought

It is the sacred and special responsibility of the community of grace – the company of people who have received the 'free gift' and whose growth in faith is dependent on that grace – to offer both the gift itself and the possibility of growth it brings to others.

A Prayer
Draw me ever nearer, O God
  to the source of power
    to the fount of grace
      to the roots of love
May I find in the Holy Spirit
  source, fount and roots
  and so be full of the life divine

                        Amen

April 8

A Thought
It is the glory of Christ that He showed the accepting, understanding attitude of God to human weakness and a proper perspective on the real seriousness of so-called sins, but He remains, nevertheless, Jesus the prophet whose searching gaze illuminates that which is false, evil and wrong, and calls for change, both personal and public.

A Prayer
I turn unfilled to You again, O God
  My need is
    great
      continual
      urgent
Out of Your infinite kindness supply my need, O God
  Let grace be
    great
      continual
      urgent
  for I need You now

                        Amen

April 9

A Thought
I like to think that Jesus may have helped the rich young ruler to understand the meaning of eternal life through His refusal to lower the demands of the Kingdom, even though He created such sorrow in the rich young man by doing it. I wonder if sometime, somewhere, the demand he could not meet became the truth that led to a change of values at the core of his life?

I hope, deeply, that there was such a redemptive moment, a response to Love.

A Prayer
O Holy Spirit
  move in me
    to take away my arrogance
    to cleanse me of my faults
    to redeem my aggressiveness
    to make new my hope
So moved by the energy and power of the Spirit
  may I offer to the world
    not righteous acts
    but true goodness

Amen

April 10

A Thought
The ability to receive of the divine giving needs to be carried over into everyday life. There is a time to give, but there is also a time to receive. Strangely enough it is often those who are most fully involved in the ministry of giving who find it hardest to accept what is there to be received.

It is so easy to land in the position of being the perpetual giver that you resent the 'weakness' of having to receive.

A Prayer
Let me walk with You, O God
  in the ways that lead to life
Show me the right path
  the good way
    the clear road
Protect me from the edge of the ravine
  the hidden danger
    the false perspective
And bring me safely to the home I seek

                    Amen

April 11

A Thought

At the heart of all pastoral work is respect for the secrets people carry. Secrets must never be dragged out or blasted out. They must be freely given. Only then is it appropriate to share secrets.

   To be entrusted with secrets is to be in a privileged position.

A Prayer
Grant, O Lord, this day
  Divine surprises
May I meet Your Son
  in the unexpected
May I trace Your presence
  in each happening
May I find Your love
  in the way things work together

                    Amen

April 12

A Thought
  'My population is too large,
  Beyond the strength of one man

I carry the whole world around,
Like a sobbing child on my back.'
So wrote the Russian poet, Yevtushenko. And so we all feel it often. It is important to do what we can. There is divine acceptance of our sincere offering, however limited it be – just as there was for the woman who 'did what she could' for Christ.

A Prayer
Lord
  In our failings
    make us penitent
  In our successes
    make us humble
  In our indecision
    give us strength
  In our decision-making
    save us from arrogance
  In ourselves
    give us peace

                    Amen

April 13

A Thought
  How awful is the pain of rejection!
  How awful it is to have to reject!

A Prayer
When all things seem against me, O Lord
  lighten my darkness
  lift my eyes
  breathe strength into me and
  bring to pass a new beginning
For we know all things work together for good
  if our love is for You

                    Amen

April 14

A Thought

It is easier to accept people with a physical disability than to accept those with mental disability. The latter, it is tacitly assumed, can get rid of their disability. How easily we become impatient with the *mentally* disabled when they, more than others, need our patience.

A Prayer
When the night is long
  and I cannot sleep
Will You, O God
  be present still
When the dawn comes
  may I awake
Ready for Your work
Eager for Your Kingdom

Amen

April 15

A Thought

Age is not easy to face but Browning's words (or Rabbi ben Ezra's) do help:
  'Grow old along with me!
    The best is yet to be
      The last of life, for which the first was made
    Our times are in His hand
    Who saith: 'A whole I planned'
      Youth shows but half; trust God: see all, nor be afraid.'

A Prayer
In facing age, O Lord
  grant me courage

When I meet infirmity
  give me strength
When my mind loses sharpness
  give me patience
When my eyes are dim
  grant me light within
So may I serve you, grace-fully
  in the eventide

                                        Amen

April 16

A Thought

The 'saved' today will not be found singing the songs of Zion separated from society. They will be, just because they have found salvation, in the streets of the city, the tents of the refugees, the transit camps of the displaced.

To be 'saved' means to be freed in a way that compels us to compassion for the world.

A Prayer
You do not slumber or sleep
  so thanks be to You, O Lord
  that 'through the long night watches'
  You are there
And 'when I awake
  I am still with Thee'

                                        Amen

April 17

A Thought

'Small is beautiful.' Schumacher's phrase has caught the imagination of many. It is indeed a word from the Lord.

We must not endorse the heresy so prevalent today that, to be valuable, things or people must be 'big'.

A Prayer
Give me the grace, O Lord
  to do more justly
  to love mercy more deeply
  to seek above all that I may
  walk more humbly
    with my God

                    Amen

April 18

A Thought
We have allowed the removal of many landmarks in our times – not buildings but principles, standards and values. Is it surprising that so often things seem to be 'out of control'?

'Remove not the ancient landmark, which thy fathers have set' (Proverbs 22:28).

A Prayer
Guide us, O Lord
  along the way of life
  through dark and stormy days
  through glad and peaceful nights
Keep our walk steady
  our eyes to the front
  our perspective sound and
  our steps sure
So may we reach our journey's end
  in peace

                    Amen

April 19

A Thought
St Teresa was an extraordinary saint! She had a habit of calling God 'His Majesty' and often complained to 'His Majesty' of

harsh treatment.

Once Teresa heard God say in response to her complaints: 'Teresa, this is how I treat my friends.' 'Which is why You have so few!' replied Teresa.

A Prayer
Grant me, O Lord
  to dream dreams
    of peace and purity
      of life and love
Grant me also
  the strength
    the discipline and
      the faith
To make those dreams come true
  in a life of
    serenity
      tranquillity and
        grace

                              Amen

April 20

A Thought

There are three kinds of fear that call for our understanding – the fear of rejection, the fear of death and the fear of damnation. Be 'moved to compassion' when you meet such fears.

A Prayer
If, by Your grace,
  I am spared the worst pains of life
Grant me the more the gift of empathy
So that I may feel what others know
  And offer a blessing

                              Amen

April 21

A Thought

Whatever we can and ought to expect by way of encouragement from others, it is an addition to and not a substitute for self-encouragement. Self-encouragement means the end of self-pity. It means fighting and fighting again to get up and to go on.

A Prayer
If ever I lose faith, O God
  renew in me
    the vision of the Lord
    the hope of salvation
    the promises of the faith
Then shall I be uplifted
  and comforted

                    Amen

April 22

A Thought

David, we read, 'encouraged himself in the Lord.'* He was no doubt re-emphasising the intrinsic faithfulness of God, but possibly there was even more than that present. He was validating a faith that believes 'all things work together for good' to those who love God.

The encouragement comes from a sense of the presence of God in all our human situations.

God is in the midst of all that happens to us and through us. Always.

A Prayer
I glory in Your presence, Lord
  It upholds me
    It benefits me
    It renews me

Be around me as a cloud of strength
  and a cloak of love

                          Amen

* *See also the entries for September 21-24 on 'The Ministry of Encouragement'.*

April 23

A Thought
There are two ways of reacting to the unacceptable situations in which we find ourselves. The first is an all-out effort to destroy the situation completely. The second is an attempt to accept, consciously and deliberately, the fact of what is, and work with it or within it.

Colonel Alida Bosshardt, evangelist extraordinary of the 'Red Light' district in Amsterdam, chose that second way and exercised for twenty-seven years, a remarkable ministry to girls whose profession she rejected but whom she loved.

A Prayer
When I have to go through tainted places
  strengthen my faith, O Lord
When I am face to face with evil
  encourage me, O Lord
When occasions for compromise face me
  make my judgement clear, O Lord

                          Amen

April 24

A Thought
Frustrated expectations can and do produce prejudice. The feelings of hostility that the religious and political leaders of Israel had towards Jesus – and which ultimately led to crucifixion – were very much

related to their inability to understand a Messiah who simply did not conform to expectations.

If we do have prejudices, it is important to look for the roots of them. Those roots may well lie in frustration of this kind.

A Prayer
I see You, O God
　in so many places
　　in the unfolding rose
　　in the laughing child
　　in the rushing wind
And I see You as You are truly seen
　in the life of Jesus
　in the love of Jesus
　in the death of Jesus
For this vision
　I give You thanks

Amen

April 25

A Thought

Let us take no pride in our prejudices or in maintaining them when there is no reason to do so. We avoid the discipline of examining our prejudices at our peril. After all, it was prejudices, fantasies and projections that crucified our Lord.

A Prayer
Grant me the grace, O God
　to examine my motives and assess my prejudices
Then give me more grace
　so that I face my weaknesses with honesty
And change what needs to be changed

Amen

April 26

A Thought

A German colleague and his wife had five children of their own and five they adopted. The second five were from the former East Berlin – refugees from the then East Germany. So in that family East and West are one, and no longer divided by a wall or anything else.

This surely is an example of reconciliation and true unity.

A Prayer
It is hard, O Lord, to be cut off
  from places you love
  from people you love
  from those you love most of all
Across the human divisions
  let there be divine oneness
Like the oneness Christ found in You

Amen

April 27

A Thought

Happy and blessed are the poor! What an extraordinary statement this is. But Jesus means it, whether we think of it as material poverty (in Luke's version of the Beatitudes) or spiritual poverty of resources (Matthew's interpretation).

To be rich endangers spiritual attention, so it is safer to be poor!

To be without spiritual resources points us to Christ.

So we are truly blessed!

A Prayer
Let me never lean
  on my own understanding, O God
But rather trust in You
  with all my heart

Amen

April 28

A Thought

Happy and blessed are the broken-hearted! It seems nonsense, but the paradox is valid. Only if you know the depth of the pain of heartbreak can you know the wonder of the peace of the Divine presence.

A Prayer
Let there be
  balm in Gilead, O God
    for every wounded soul

                    Amen

April 29

A Thought

  Blessed are the persecuted!

  Can this be?

  It can be, because the need for people to 'persecute' you for righteousness' sake, testifies to the effectiveness of your life and witness.

  Be happy if this privilege is yours!

A Prayer
Give me, O God
  Calm when I am surrounded by stress
  Serenity if I am under strain
  Peace as pressures bear down on me
  Tranquillity when I am in travail
So may I always be
  in balance
And of greater use
  in Your service

                    Amen

April 30

A Thought

Grace has to do with *giving* and *gift*. It is a very particular kind of giving in a very specific 'gift relationship'. It is a giving that is totally voluntary on the part of the giver, totally uninvited on the part of the receiver, wholly without any implicit obligation on the part of the giver and wholly without explicit obligation on the part of the recipient.

A Prayer
O Lord, bring me
  to the end of each day
    each week
    each month
    each year
  with a sense of gratitude for blessings
    a sense of penitence for failures
    a sense of peace through forgiveness
  And as each new day, week, month, year dawns
    grant me a sense of expectation
      and hope
Through Jesus Christ, our Lord

                    Amen

MAY

Good News-points

May 1

A Thought

'I have good news for you.' The words come from the story of the angels singing to the shepherds on the hills above Bethlehem at the time of the 'first Christmas' (Luke 2:10, *New English Bible*). That message can be the printed as well as the spoken message of the church to the community.

Let no one despise the possibility of proclamation through the humble parish pamphlet, prepared and delivered in concern and with consistency.

'Tell it out...'

A Prayer
What I cannot say in words, O God
  help me to say in other ways
    in the things I write
    in the feelings I show
    in the attitudes I offer
    in the example I give
So may my witness be
  in many ways
    to many people
Through Jesus Christ, our Lord

                    Amen

May 2

A Thought

Events are ideas incarnate. The danger of settling for the *status quo* is inherent in us all. If we let it settle in, we shall lose hope. Let there be life!

We cannot change the world overnight or even over a lifetime, but we have the power to encourage and to effect change in little ways if our expectations for life are real and we have living hope.

A Prayer
Grant me the ability, O God
to see beneath events
and discern reality
to see beneath human exteriors
and find the soul
to have insight into life
and so to help
To be used as a means of healing
and so to bless

Amen

May 3

A Thought
'What thou seest, write in a book, and send it...' (Revelation 1:11). Truth needs the playwright with his offering of words in action. Truth needs the controversialist. Truth needs the thinker and his thoughts. Truth needs the poet, for the poet too can say 'I have some good news for you' in a way that reaches the inner being.

A Prayer
I want to give to You
I want to fight for You
I want to labour for You
I want to serve You
Teach me, O Lord, how to do this
And grant me the grace to do it

Amen

May 4

A Thought

It is always a mistake to give universal authority to an idea which, though of value in itself, is only an aid to understanding and is only a part that cannot be the whole. Paul Tillich confirms this when he says of one such approach: 'It elevates something finite and transitory to infinite and eternal validity.'

We make this mistake at our peril.

A Prayer
If this be a day of gladness
  I praise You, O God
If this be a day of sadness
  I seek You, O God
If this be a day of challenge
  I lean on You, O God
If this be a day of achievement
  I thank You, O God

                              Amen

May 5

A Thought

In Christian communication, we all too easily assume that all church members read 'serious' journals such as (in Britain), *The Times*, the *Daily Telegraph* or the *Guardian* whereas the reality is that the vast majority read the 'populars' like the *Sun*, the *Star* and the *Daily Mirror*. Much of our 'communication' is too intellectual.

There is a great opportunity today for 'communicators' who can convey truth in simple words. We need that ministry of print.

A Prayer
I offer You my words of praise, O God
  Hear my thanks
I offer You my silence, O God

Speak to me in Your still, small voice
I offer You my activity, O God
  Bless my strenuous endeavours
I offer You myself, O God
  Bless me

                       Amen

May 6

A Thought

'Write down therefore what you have seen, what is now, and what will be hereafter' (Revelation 1:19, *New English Bible*).

You have good news to give. Speak, write, live it to His glory.

A Prayer
When I am at the end of my tether
  when all things are against me
Grant me, O God
  the patience to wait
    the faith to believe
      the trust to obey
So shall I find the peace I need
  to survive and to go on

                       Amen

May 7

A Thought

We need true prophets. Not soothsayers, astrologers, wizards but true prophets. For prophets are those who see behind the form to the thought, behind the events to the significance, behind the actions to the motives.

Call in the prophets!

A Prayer
You speak within us, O Lord, so
  help us to hear

You smile upon us, O Lord, so
  help us to laugh
You breathe Your Spirit through us, O Lord, so
  help us to love
You make us new, O Lord, so
  help us to bless

Amen

May 8

A Thought

'A quest,' says Father Louis Marteau (in his book, *Words of Counsel*) 'is an on-going action where the final answer may never be discovered but where fulfilment is derived from the quest itself.'

Enjoy exploring!

A Prayer
Grant, O Lord
  that my life be a
  Spiral of Renewal
  at all times

Amen

May 9

A Thought

'You sat on a mountain top in the East for as long as you liked and it was perfectly all right with everyone in the neighbourhood. In the West they pick you up for vagrancy.' Different worlds!

A Prayer
Grant me a sense of humour, O Lord
  for there is a time to laugh
Grant me a sympathy with sorrow, O Lord
  for there is a time to weep

Grant me a voice of praise, O Lord
  for there is a time to sing
Grant me a soul with faith, O Lord
  for there is a time to pray

                              Amen

May 10

A Thought

The danger of confusing liberty with licence is always present for Christians. But the position is clear, freedom involves not anarchy but discipline.

Grace does not allow us to do what we like. It enables us to do 'as God likes' in a way that we could not do it before.

A Prayer
May Your Son live in me, O God
  determining my attitudes
  deciding my choices
  directing my thinking
So may I live in Christ
and He in me

                              Amen

May 11

A Thought

Comfort and challenge are not opposites. They are rather complementary to each other. The Gospel is both a challenge and a comfort.

It would not help us if all we ever got was comfort, or if all were challenge.

We need both – together.

A Prayer
'O strengthen me,

that while I stand
Firm on the rock and strong in Thee
I may stretch out a loving hand
To wrestlers with the troubled sea'

Amen

(Words by Frances Ridley Havergal)

May 12

A Thought

Billy Graham *did* sometimes comment on the problems of the world – as I recalled when I read a letter from him to me. It was written in 1964 with relation to racialism. He says: 'My conviction is that the problem will not be solved by demonstrations which are becoming increasingly violent. Nor will it be solved by Laws. It must come from the hearts of the people who have swept out prejudice and hate. In my opinion, this can come about only by education and the transforming power of the Gospel of Christ.'

A Prayer
Lord, in all my journeying
may I look forward
for the best is yet to be
may I look outward
for the exploration of the unknown is exciting
may I look upward
for 'without Thee I can do nothing'

Amen

May 13

A Thought

Christian truth is conveyed through relationship, example, influence, intellect, imagination, Word, Sacrament, symbol, image, meditation, worship, and so on.

Whichever way is our way, let us use it to the full.

A Prayer
Let me not be intolerant, O Lord
  demanding that my way be 'the' way
Let me rather give freedom to others
  to find the way best for themselves
So shall I contribute to conviction
  and the confirmation of the truth

                    Amen

May 14

A Thought

The long search for the spiritual goes on. But, like so much in life, it has two sides. It can lead to seeking and finding that which is good or it can easily keel over and find itself involved in the dark side of life.

We need the 'good news' in every form – sermon, song, symbol, print, poetry, play – if we are to tip the balance of the life of the world to the 'good side'.

A Prayer
What I can give
  let me give freely, O God
My personal talents
  my thoughts and insights
    my perceptions and
      my understanding
For dedicated to Your purpose
  All that I have however small
    can be of use in Your kingdom

                    Amen

May 15

A Thought

Symbols can become idols, and fear of that (with historical reason) has led to less use than is right of symbolism in some branches of the church. But people need symbols. They need the focal point that has meaning and will take their imagination to the truths that lie beyond the symbols.

A Prayer
Help me, O Lord
  so to set my sights
    that, naturally, I
      do justly
        love mercy
          and walk humbly with You
    that, naturally, I
    seek first Your Kingdom
      and its righteousness
        love You and my neighbour
          hold fast to that which is good

                              Amen

May 16

A Thought

Poetry has a capacity to reach the depths of a person's being in a way that rational appeal cannot. It is, because of this, a real means of communication and should be used much more.

A Prayer
I thank You, O God
  for the true and the lovely
    for melody and music
    for poetry and poems
    for art and pictures
  for dance and grace

Through them may I learn more of the beauty
  that is divine

                                        Amen

May 17

A Thought

Poetry, because it belongs to the world of symbols and images, is directed particularly towards the imagination. Its impact, even when not wholly understood at the rational, intellectual level, is felt at the emotional and spiritual levels. It has the capacity to reach the depths of a person's being in a way that rational appeal just cannot do. Poetry touches, in Gerard Manley Hopkins' phrase, 'deep-down things'.

A Prayer
Minister to me, O God
  in the deep reaches of my soul
Cast out my faults
  through Your grace
Cast out my fear
  through Your love
Cast out my anxious thought
  through Your peace

                              Amen

May 18

A Thought

How marvellous are the 'myths' of Genesis! The story of the Fall of Adam and Eve in the Garden of Eden is so symbolic of the disintegration which disobedience to God brings. It brought disharmony between man and woman, between man and beast (3:15), in nature ('thorns and thistles', verse 18), humanity and God. Complete disintegration!

How marvellous that 'a second Adam to the fight and to the rescue came.'

A Prayer
Restore to me, O Lord
the joy of Your salvation
the relationship of love I so constantly break
the peace the world cannot give
the life that is abundant

Amen

May 19

A Thought

Paul Tillich has written a book called *On the Boundary*. He is thinking of many boundaries on which he had to live – city and country, reality and imagination, religion and culture, and so on. Such living involved creative tensions for him.

A Prayer
When I survey 'the wondrous Cross'
I count my richest gains as loss
May I trust only in my Lord
and find my joy in serving Him

Amen

May 20

A Thought

We 'live on the boundary' between two worlds – this world and the world that is spiritual. We have therefore (Jesus said) to be 'in' but not 'of' the world.

Living in such a way therefore makes necessary (to repeat phrases I have used before) 'retreat' and 'involvement', 'detachment' and 'participation'. But this was indeed the essence of the Incarnation.

A Prayer
Give us the insight, O Lord
  to live in the world of now
  on the standards of the world to come
Give us the faith, O Lord
  to believe in eternal reality while
  we live in temporal unreality
Give us the peace, O Lord
  that comes from such creative tension

                            Amen

May 21

A Thought

Intuitionally man has always been ahead of his scientific and technological discoveries. Phenomena known for centuries to mystics, saints and psychics are now being found to be open to scientific discovery. This should encourage us to trust our intuitions. Some of our intuitions are no more than imagination, fantasy and wishful thinking that is part of our so-called unconscious, but there are prophetic intuitions and experiences not verifiable scientifically that are very important.

Test the spirits, we are told. Test, too, our intuitions.

A Prayer
Help me, O Lord
  to look within myself and
    be honest and ready to face what is there
  to look below the surface of others
    and be ready to accept what is there
  to look below events and happenings and
    be ready to interpret what I find
  to look behind the outward forms and
    be ready to sense the reality beyond them

                            Amen

May 22

A Thought

Tony Monopoly, who was a monk in a contemplative order before he became a pop singer, says it is essential that a monk should have a sense of humour! He also says that he was able to cope with the commitments to 'poverty' and 'chastity', but that 'obedience' was quite another matter. To be asked to give up his freedom was just too much.

But is not Christian obedience true liberty? 'Make me a captive Lord, and *then* I shall be free.'

A Prayer
Grant me, O Lord
  the liberation that comes through Your Spirit
  so that I may not be imprisoned
    by legalism
      by guilt
        by habit
Never let me make my liberty into licence but
Help me to find in true liberty
  the freedom to be, with gladness

                    Amen

May 23

A Thought

Disorder is never a mark of the Spirit. There is 'balance' and order in everything the Spirit does. The gift of discernment has a part to play where so-called gifts of the Spirit are being expressed. It is the gift that tests the spirits and every manifestation they produce to see if they are 'of God'.

Keep lively the gift of discernment.

A Prayer
Move in me, O Lord
  in mysterious ways
   Your wonders to perform
Flow silently and subtly
  through my being
Conscious and unconscious
Till the whole of me is
  the temple of Your Spirit

Amen

May 24

A Thought

The doctrine of 'money' is much raised these days. May I offer my credo on it, after a long and varied experience?

Giving freely, without counting the cost, has done nothing but produce for me 'divine surprises' and 'added blessings'.

A Prayer
May rest be Your gift to the weary
May joy be Your gift to the sad
May Your light shine in our darkness
May Your peace dwell in our souls
  So may Your power strengthen us
  and Your love embrace us

Amen

May 25

A Thought

'Foxes have holes and birds of the air have nests. But the Son of Man hath not where to lay His head.'

Jesus sat lightly on money and possessions, not because they are not necessary, but because, in true priorities, they are very much in second place.

A Prayer
Let me have no 'anxious thoughts'
  about tomorrow
But quietly go my way
  aware of Your loving-kindness
Help me always, to
  seek first Your Kingdom and its righteousness
  leaving 'other things', quietly and confidently
  to be 'added' in Your tender mercy
Thus may we have the attitude to life
  that Your Son, Jesus, had

Amen

May 26

A Thought
A sensible diet, an alert and steady mind, and devotion to universal law sounds good contemporary sense. In fact, this advice comes from Inhotep, a priest-physician in Egypt around 3000 BC!

There is nothing new under the sun, but there is modern wisdom which is really very ancient. And where ancient and modern coincide despite some 5,000 years between, it is probable that we are touching a universal truth.

A Prayer
Lord
  when I am harassed
    give me peace
  when I am under pressure
    keep me calm
  Enable me to preserve my serenity
    by taking a day at a time
  Enable me to radiate tranquillity
    by resting in You

Amen

May 27

A Thought
The current violence and vandalism of society shows a lack of respect for property – and people too. The respect old age has traditionally demanded has also near disappeared. The privacies that used to be – in deep relationship or personal failure –are exposed in the name of openness, and 'private life' having ceased as a right, is criticised as a fault.

It is inevitable that respect for the divine and the sacred suffers in the same process. Respect for God has gone with loss of respect for people.

A Prayer
Let my light so shine before men
  that they may see my good works
    and glorify my Father which is in heaven

                                    Amen

May 28

A Thought
The late Hugo Gryn, the well-known Rabbi, went through awful experiences in Auschwitz. A particular sentence he used in the television programme *In the Light of Experience* is profoundly haunting: 'Auschwitz is an example of what can happen when technology is harnessed to evil.'
It is.

A Prayer
Deliver us, O Lord
  from the sin that clouds our vision
  from the hate that dims our perception
  from the subtlety that rationalises our failures
  from the evil that is part of our lot
Create in us only that which is good

                                    Amen

May 29

A Thought

'Style,' said Dr Roy Strong, 'is adding to the art of life.'

A Prayer
May the music of the spheres
  be reflected in the music of my soul, O Lord
May the drama of the world
  be felt through the traumas of my heart, O Lord
May the art of the artist and the poetry of the poets, O Lord
  touch the hidden springs in me
And so add to my life, O Lord

                    Amen

May 30

A Thought

'I believe in the fullest utilisation of each fleeting day,' wrote Jomo Kenyatta (in *Suffering without Bitterness*). He goes on: 'Of all the deadly sins, that of sloth seems to me the most contemptible, a flaunting of the very purpose of Creation.'

A Prayer
Send me, O Lord, on Your business
Support me, when I fail in it
Comfort me, when the road is rough
Lift me up, when I fall
And when something of good is done by someone
Share with me Your joy

                    Amen

May 31
A Thought
And now hallelujah! the rest of my days
Shall gladly be spent in promoting His praise

Who opened His bosom to pour out this sea
Of boundless salvation for you and for me.*

A Prayer
Let Your love, O God
  like the mighty ocean waves
    roll over me
So that I may be
  engulfed in grace
Through Jesus Christ, our Lord

                    Amen

* quoted in *HERE IS MY HAND*. It is one of the inspirational pieces in the room of Colonel Alida Bosshardt, subject of that book by Denis Duncan. Colonel Bosshardt served as a Salvation Army officer in the Red Light District of Amsterdam for 27 years.

JUNE

Deep-down Things

June 1

A Thought

'Deep is calling to deep' sings the Psalmist (42:7). It is out of our depths we cry: it is out of God's depths, He responds.

In the meeting of the depths, there is always the possibility of miracle.

A Prayer
Lord, I cry to You
  in my need, for I am frail
  in my guilt, for I do fail
  in my penitence, for I do grieve
  in my expectation, for I would receive
Grant me the gifts You promise
  and all I need will be mine
Through Jesus Christ, our Lord

Amen

June 2

A Thought

It is as true of things spiritual, as of the Bible and of the Faith, that 'the deeper you dig, the more you will find.'

A Prayer
Search me, O God
  and know my thoughts
Create in me, a clean heart, O God
Renew a right spirit within me
Restore to me the joy of Your salvation
Uphold me with Your free Spirit

O Lord, open my lips and
  my mouth shall show forth Your praise
                                    Amen

June 3

A Thought
'Leisure,' writes Mother Mary Clare in her book of that title, 'is part of the process of the re-creation of Christ.'

In that connection she quotes an unusual rendering of Psalm 46:10: 'Have leisure and know that I am God.'

A Prayer
Be still, my soul
  the Lord is on Your side
Be still, my soul
  the Lord is your shepherd
Be still, my soul
  Jesus lives!
Be still, my soul
  In Jesus Christ our Lord

                                    Amen

June 4

A Thought
'Nature,' G. L. Playfair and Scott Hill write in *Cycles of Heaven*, 'unlike universities, is not divided into faculties, departments and sub-departments. It is not divided into anything. It is one whole.'

A Prayer
Turn my eyes, O God
  on Your Son, Jesus
So that 'looking full on His wonderful face
  The cares of earth may grow strangely dim
  in the light of His glory and grace'

                                    Amen

June 5

A Thought

Roberta Miller, whom to meet was an inspiration, writes: 'The Universe is in perfect order, not a thing out of place. From the viewpoint of cosmic equilibrium there is a reason for every event.'

There is a great truth within that statement.

A Prayer
Make me aware, Lord, of
  the Hand that guides me
  the Feet that lead me
  the Strength that upholds me
  the Love that surrounds me

Amen

June 6

A Thought

The healing of the soul, the self, is so much more than the restitution of the body. Indeed the acceptance that physical healing cannot always be given, may, in itself, be transformed into a ministry to the whole person.

For those in the depths of pain, this is a hard saying. What I say, however, I say on the testimony of those who have suffered a great deal.

A Prayer
Thanks be to You, O Lord
  for the witness of the good who suffer and show through their suffering
    Your divine presence
    Your redeeming grace
    Your transforming power
May their example be my inspiration

Amen

June 7

A Thought

We only see through a glass darkly so our touching of the divine is but an inkling of the reality that is to be. But of that reality, we have, in fleeting moments of heightened awareness, intuitional experiences.

That experience is objectively confirmed in the history of the saints.

A Prayer
Grant, O God, that
  dreaming dreams and
  seeing visions
I may turn thought into event
  and idea into reality
And so creatively bless the world

Amen

June 8

A Thought

I am sure that one of the most profoundly important sayings in the Bible is this: 'Perfect love banishes fear' (1 John 4:18, *New English Bible*).

A Prayer
Fill me, O God, with
  initiative
    energy
      enthusiasm
        faith
So may I climb mountains of doubt
  walk boldly through valleys of decision
    skip lightly over hindrances and obstacles and
      run happily on the way to life

Amen

June 9

A Thought
The first thing Zacchaeus had to do when he met Jesus was, as St. Luke tells us in his Gospel (19:5), to 'come down' to him. It was, literally, a necessity, but the action is symbolically significant too. The first step on the way to salvation and wholeness – as St Paul had to find out too – is so often a 'climb-down' process, a realisation of our need to understand that, in matters of the soul, we can, of ourselves, do nothing. Only grace is 'sufficient' for us.

A Prayer
Dwell in me, O Lord
that the world may know that
I have 'been with Jesus'
So may my light shine before men
and glorify Your name

Amen

June 10

A Thought
'First the blade, then the ear, then the full corn in the ear.' This statement which is about evolution is a chapter heading in a book about the famous Henry Drummond (who wrote *The Greatest Thing in the World*).

In spiritual terms, 'revolution' is the more important word, for only after 'revolution' (that is conversion or justification) can 'evolution' (that is growth in grace or sanctification) take place.

A Prayer
Bring me, O God
to decision
to surrender
to obedience

Then produce in me the fruit of the Spirit
  to the Glory of Your Name
                                    Amen

June 11

A Thought

Francis McNutt writes (in *Healing*): 'The simple and the poor followed Jesus in crowds because they saw what happened. The religious leaders tried to figure out what it all meant.'

It is like the man who said to the 'theorising' Pharisees: 'Whether He be a sinner or no, I know not: one thing I know, that whereas I was blind, now I see' (John 9:25).

Faith is trusting acceptance rather than logical deduction.

A Prayer
Grant me, O Lord
  eyes to see
    ears to hear
      a heart to feel and
        a mind to embrace
the 'inklings of eternity' that break through into life
                                    Amen

June 12

A Thought

"It is more blessed to give than to receive." It is also easier – for many.

This is not a reason to stop giving. It is simply a reminder about the need to receive gratefully *and* graciously, whatever the gift.

A Prayer
Stay with me, Lord
  in pain
    in puzzlement
      in panic
Let Your continuing Presence be
  my guide and stay
    always

                          Amen

June 13

A Thought

There is always co-operation in spiritual achievement. Without God we can do nothing – that is primary. But while it is God who works in us in the re-creation of our lives, we must then co-operate with God by 'working out our own salvation.'

Two are (as the Old Testament preacher reminds us) 'better than one' – especially if one of them is God.

A Prayer
Jesus, Thou joy of loving hearts
  I turn unfilled to You
Make up all I lack
  in faith
    in hope
      in love
So that my whole life be
  an offering You can receive and use

                          Amen

June 14

A Thought

Self-awareness is but the preparation for the gift of the 'grace of our Lord Jesus Christ.' Repentance, in Christian terms, is always the preliminary to 'justification' and its expression in spiritual growth, 'sanctification'.

We cannot repent unless we are 'self-aware': aware that is of our state of need; aware of our empathy with the cry of the heart Paul uttered as he contemplated 'the good that I would' that is not done and 'the evil that I would not' that is. 'Who shall deliver me from the body of this death?' he cries in desperation.

His answer is the Christian answer for all time.

'I thank God, through Jesus Christ, my Lord.'

A Prayer
Graciously keep me on the right path, O God
Graciously keep my eye in the right direction
Graciously encourage me to go forward
Graciously enable me to attain to life

Amen

June 15

A Thought

Affluence breeds spiritual danger. It *is* hard for a rich man to enter the Kingdom of God. Sophistication kills the simplicity that is required in discipleship. 'Except ye be converted and become as little children, ye shall not enter the Kingdom of God.'

The spiritual life demands that 'the normal' so far as the world is concerned be abandoned in order to find 'the real'.

A Prayer
Help me to value
the simple and the natural things, O God
the gift of daily bread
the glory of nature
the song of the birds
the cry of a child
So may I find I have the things that matter most

Amen

June 16

A Thought

At the very point in history when mankind is beginning to learn that 'man does not live by bread alone', the churches have been found wanting, not because of their unwillingness, their hostility or their ineffectiveness, but because they sometimes seem to have lost their treasure.

We cannot offer the spiritual depths to others unless and until we re-discover them for ourselves.

A Prayer
Give me the grace, O God
  to understand the mysteries of faith
  and to interpret them to others
So may I be blessed with
  'the knowledge beyond knowledge' myself
    and be used to make it known to others

                    Amen

June 17

A Thought

St Teresa is another who stresses true freedom in the Spirit. 'Whatever moves us in such a way as to feel that our reason is not free, should be looked on as suspicious.'

A Prayer
Set Your seal, O Lord
  on all that has been done for Your glory today
Go before us into tomorrow
  illumining the path with Your light
So may we miss no opportunity
  to serve You with all our hearts

                    Amen

June 18

A Thought

'Lord, is it I?' This was the question each disciple asked Jesus when He said: 'One of you shall betray me.'

When we worry about our failure to be good servants of God, it is a comfort to realise the church was founded and built on a group of men who *all* felt it to be possible that they had betrayed Jesus.

A Prayer
When failure is hard to bear
  comfort me, O Lord
When success is hard to realise
  reassure me, O Lord
When consistency is hard to create
  strengthen me, O Lord
When constancy is achieved,
  I bless you, O Lord

                    Amen

June 19

A Thought

Holy worldliness implies both 'involvement' and 'distance'. 'Worldliness' is the involvement. 'Holiness' implies distance.

It is not the Christian's function to opt out of the world. As with Christ Himself, the only possible place is within it. It is the Christian's responsibility to realise the call to holiness and accept the true apartness involved.

The recovery of apartness and, in that sense, holiness, must be a discipline for all who seek to grow in grace. It is so much easier to be 'worldly' than to be 'holy'.

A Prayer
When tension fills my body
  grant me, O God, Your peace

Let peace, like a river, flow through me
  bringing relaxation, rest and regeneration
So may I be renewed in body and soul

                              Amen

June 20

A Thought

Irresponsibility is indefensible. Responsibility is dull. But 'creative irresponsibility' is another matter. It refers to those who, for creative purposes, undertake initiatives which involve risk, but who are prepared to see them through to success.

The 'irresponsibility' element lies in their being operations that no 'responsible' person would risk. The risk taken, very creative things can happen.

A Prayer
O Lord
  When the pressures of each day bear down
    on troubled mind and anxious soul
  'Breathe through' my cares and concern
    'Thy coolness and Thy balm'
Anoint my mind with the
  'oils of tranquillity'
Through 'images of stillness'
  restore serenity to my soul

                              Amen

June 21

A Thought

We shall not always be heard for our 'babbling on' (Matthew 6:7, *New English Bible*). Words have their place – we must 'ask' in order to 'receive' (Matthew 7:7). But let not the command to be 'importunate' in our prayers lead us into a dependence on words that may blind us to the need for silence.

A Prayer
In my loneliness
  be a Presence
In my sadness
  be a Comfort
In my joy
  be my Companion
In my pain
  be my Physician

                    Amen

June 22

A Thought
Grace has to do with growth. It is not only the ground of justification. It is the guarantee of sanctification. And what is sanctification but growing in faith and into the wholeness of the spiritual life?

A Prayer
When I worry about tomorrow, O God
  make me aware of Your faithfulness today
So shall I learn that I may depend
  on Your Divine Consistency
And be at peace

                    Amen

June 23

A Thought
Temptation does not disappear, suddenly or gradually, from the life in process of spiritual growth. Particular temptations may change but the severity of temptation will become greater and continue to increase, in a profound sense, until life's end.

   We do not cease to need grace, or need it less, as we grow into faith. We need it more.

A Prayer
May grace, mercy and peace
be mine this day

Amen

June 24

A Thought

The Bible is full of invitations!
'Come unto Me...'
'O taste and see that the Lord is good'
'Whosoever cometh, I will in no wise cast out'
'Ask...'
'Seek...'
'Knock...'
And there are so many more.
RSVP!
Accept!

A Prayer
Make known to me, O God
The Love that 'came down at Christmas'
Make real in me, O God
The Love that 'came down at Christmas'
Fill me with that Love Divine
  Now and always

Amen

June 25

A Thought

'*Come* unto me, all ye that labour and are heavy laden, and I will give you rest.' '*Go* ye into all the world.' Christianity is real and full when both of these things are happening, paradoxically, together!

A Prayer
Give me the grace to come to You, O God
  acknowledging my need
Give me the strength to go, O God
  offering Your love
So, in my coming in and my going out
  may I praise Your name
    evermore

Amen

June 26

A Thought

We need more careful thinking, not less; more theology, not less, if there is to be effective ministry today. The proper modern emphasis on the importance of feeling is not a denial of the intellect but an effort to correct an imbalance that has damaged the faith. We need feeling and thinking as co-operators, not enemies.

A Prayer
Take my mind, O God
  and give it insight
Take my feelings, O God
  and give them depth
Take my motives, O God
  and keep them pure
Take my will, O God
  and make it Yours

Amen

June 27

A Thought

'When in His infinite mercy, God creates new man out of the old man,' writes Sonia Syner, 'He brings him to birth; He brings him to his feet; He brings him to his senses; He brings him to his knees; He brings him to himself as God meant him to be; He brings him to Christ in him, and so into brotherhood with all humanity. He brings him to the Kingdom, and there, wholly re-created by the power of God, the Father, wholly liberated through the love of Christ the Son and perpetually re-kindled at the flame of the Holy Spirit, he learns with ever-deepening wonder, awe and adoration of his own oneness with the Godhead, and with every living thing.'

A Prayer
Teach me, O Lord
  how to be one with You
  and so to be at one with humanity
  in unity with Your Spirit
    make me strong to grasp what is the breadth, length
    height and depth of the love of Christ
      and so to find my peace

Amen

June 28

A Thought

'Never go ahead of God's providence,' said Vincent de Paul. But he added that once we know what God wants us to do, there must be no turning back and no letting up. But take it at God's speed. 'I shall walk in the pace of my Lord,' as the twenty-third Psalm (Japanese version) reminds us. 'The Lord is our Pace-Setter.'

A Prayer
As with gladness men of old
  did the guiding star behold
May I gladly follow the star each day
  finding Bethlehem's worship

seeing more clearly that which came to pass
  in Bethlehem of long ago
committed to give myself, my gift

                              Amen

June 29

A Thought
  I know not what the future hath
    Of marvel or surprise;
  Assured alone that, life and death,
    His mercy underlies.
  I know not where His islands lift
    Their fronded palms to air;
  I only know I cannot drift
    Beyond His love and care*

A Prayer
Make me a channel of your peace
  It is in pardoning that we are pardoned
    in giving to all men that we receive
And in dying that we are born to eternal life

                              Amen

(based on words by Sebastian Temple)
(words by John Greenleaf Whittier)*

June 30

A Thought
  All my days and all my hours
  All my will and all my powers
  All the passion of my soul
  Not a fragment, but the whole
    Shall be Thine, dear Lord.

A Prayer
Grant me, O God
  energy for the day
    sleep for the night
      rest for body and mind
        renewal for heart and soul
Then shall I be ready
  to serve You again
  a day at a time
Through Jesus Christ, our Lord

Amen

JULY

Firm Foundations

July 1

A Thought

These are three benedictions in Psalm 84:

Blessed is the one whose Joy is in God (verses 1-4)

Blessed is the one whose Strength is in God (verses 5-8)

Blessed is the one whose Trust is in God (verses 9-12)

Joy, Strength and Trust 'in God' make for true inner Peace.

A Prayer
  Grant me, O Lord
  Time for Thought
  Space for Solitude
  Room for Reflection
  and a Place for Prayer
So may I be renewed daily
  Through Jesus Christ, our Lord
                      Amen

July 2

A Thought

How often Jesus uses the word 'must' – of what He has to do.

'I *must* be about my Father's business' (Luke 2:49)

'I *must* preach the Kingdom of God' (Luke 4:43)

'I *must* work the works of Him that sent me' (John 9:4)

'Them also I *must* bring' (John 10:16)

'Today I *must* abide at thy house' (Luke 19:5)

'The Son of man *must* be lifted up' (John 12:34)

The pressure that comes in the word 'must', in each case, had to do with the will of God. Treat with respect an inner sense that says 'you must'. It involves conviction *and* commitment for *you*.

A Prayer
I bless You, O Lord, for
  New mercies given
  Old weaknesses accepted
  Fresh opportunities offered
  Love, unchanging, received
Help me always, in grateful response, to press toward the mark for the
prize of the high calling of God in Christ Jesus

Amen

July 3

A Thought
Are you depressed by temptation, overwhelmed with failure, despondent over growth in grace? Be comforted. Father Andrew reminds us of the universality of such feelings in *In the Silence*. 'It is the testimony of all the saints from the beginning,' he writes, 'that the spiritual life is a combat.' It is but we are never left to battle alone.

A Prayer
In the mysteries of life, O Lord
  Grant us
  Infinite trust
  Calm confidence
  Profound insight
  Inexhaustible hope
Then may we find that, loving You, all things do truly work together
for good

Amen

July 4

A Thought
Three gardens of the Bible speak to us –
  Eden, the Garden of Creation
  Gethsemane, the Garden of Dereliction

The Garden of the Resurrection
Life *is* Creation, Dereliction and Resurrection together.

A Prayer
Forgive my 'foolish ways', O God
  and make me wise
If 'fool' I must be
  let it be only 'for Christ's sake'
And in such 'foolishness'
  may Yours be the glory

Amen

July 5

A Thought
Do not worry if growth in grace is slow. 'We should be the "waiting ones",' writes Sister Eva of Friedenshort. 'The "work of transfiguration" is one that goes forward gradually.'

A Prayer
Looking back, may I be filled with gratitude
Looking forward, may I be filled with hope
Looking upward, may I be conscious of strength
Looking inward, may I find deep peace

Amen

July 6

A Thought
There is a marvellous statement by the great preacher P. T Forsyth. He writes:

'I should count a life well spent, and the world well lost, if after tasting all its experiences and facing all its problems, I had no more to show, at its close, or to carry to another life, than the acquisition of a real, sure, humble and grateful faith in the eternal and incarnate Son of God.'

A Prayer
Peace be with me
  awake
  asleep
  by day in toil
  by night in rest
Peace be with me
  always

Amen

July 7

A Thought
  'This is the business of our life
  By effort and toil
  By prayer and supplication
  To advance in the Grace of God'
So wrote St. Augustine.

A Prayer
Let the note of joy
be in my undertakings
Let the note of faith
be in my living
Let the note of hope
be in my dying
Let the gift of peace
be always with me

Amen

July 8

A Thought
Meddling with the psychic is not profitable, but a deep involvement

with that more profound dimension – the spiritual – is. Only as we are in touch with the spiritual and affected by it, can we reach both the profundity of the faith and the harvest that follows from such contact. It is in the deep places that we meet God.

A Prayer
Take me, O Lord
  to where I shall meet with You
Lead me, O Lord
  in ways of holiness and righteousness
Guide me, O Lord
  to the hidden springs of faith
Bring me, O Lord
  to knowledge of the Truth in Christ Jesus
So may I have a happy journey's end

                                    Amen

July 9

A Thought
Look to the day for its life
  the very life of life
In its brief course lie all its realities
  and truths of existence –
    The joy of growth
    The splendour of action
    The glory of power
For yesterday is but a memory
  and tomorrow is only a vision
But today, well-lived, makes every
  yesterday a memory of happiness
  and every tomorrow a vision of life
Look well therefore to this day.
So runs an ancient Sanskrit poem.

A Prayer
Make this day, O Lord, a day
  of generous giving
  and gracious receiving
  of blessings offered
  and blessings added
  of joy outflowing
  and joy experienced
So may the day end
  with deep peace and satisfaction

Amen

July 10

A Thought
We are – as Rod McKuen reminds us – 'Children one and all'. Child-like qualities (as distinct from childishness) will be, not our shame, but our joy for 'except you become as a little child, you cannot enter the Kingdom of God.' There is a 'holy innocence' which is an attribute of true faith. God grant us the child-like heart!

A Prayer
Help me, O Lord
  to be child-like
  in simple trust
  in holy innocence
  in spontaneous intuition
  in acceptance of miracle
So may I more nearly
  enter Your Kingdom

Amen

July 11

A Thought
There are two phrases in William Barclay's rendering of the first letter of Peter

that are quite memorable. First he speaks of Christians as 'exiles of eternity' and sums up beautifully just where our abiding home is. Then he describes disciples as those 'who are travelling on the road to holiness in the power of the Spirit'.

What a pilgrimage!

A Prayer
You are, O God, the
  rest of the weary
  joy of the sad
  hope of the dreary
  light of the glad
May rest and joy and hope and light
  be Your gifts to me

                              Amen

July 12

A Thought

It is acknowledgement, not attainment, that leads to life. It is the act of receiving, not the fact of deserving that restores relationship. This is the Gospel, the Good News to sorely troubled souls, who seek inner peace. It is not in the strain and stress of the spiritual struggle against the odds, nor is it in the need to please, to satisfy 'the Divine potentate', that salvation lies. It lies in the acceptance of a gift.

A Prayer
Let joy be natural to me, O Lord
  so that I uplift others
Let enthusiasm never die within me, O Lord
  so that I inspire others
Let enterprise be my mark, O Lord
  so that I contribute to Divine surprises
Let peace be my gift, O Lord
  so that I add to the peace of others
                              Amen

July 13

A Thought

In the parish church at Long Melford in Suffolk, England, there is the famous Rabbit window, depicting three rabbits. Each has two ears, but there are only three between them. The guide book suggests that this is a symbol of the Trinity.

The doctrine of the Trinity is a word-mystery, but the doctrine itself is an expression, in theological terms, of our human experience of the one God who comes to us in three ways – as Father, Christ and in the Holy Spirit. Yet there is and can be only one God.

The doctrine is a statement of what Christians know, by faith, to be reality.

A Prayer
My mind is too small, O God
  to comprehend Your greatness
But I feel Your presence
  every passing hour
So I rest in peace
  then go my way

                    Amen

July 14

A Thought

It is worth remembering at the beginning or end of each day Teilhard de Chardin's familiar words: 'All that really matters is devotion to something bigger than ourselves.'

A Prayer
Holy, holy, holy
  Lord God Almighty
Heaven and earth are
  full of Your Glory
I praise You, O God

I acknowledge You to be my Lord
And with all the earth
I worship You
Father everlasting

Amen

July 15

A Thought

The witness of the Bible in its entirety is to a relationship damaged by the sin of man in the beginning and to the possibility of relationship restored in the fullness of time. That witness includes consistent emphasis on the inability of man, on his own initiative or by his own effort, to make good the damage done through his pride, wilfulness and arrogance. That same witness points in only one direction to the divine solution. 'By grace you are saved through faith.'

A Prayer
You are 'the Lord of all being, throned afar'
  Yet to each loving heart,
    You are so near
You are the Creator of heaven and earth
  Yet to each child of God
    You are 'Our Father'
Thanks be to You, O God
  for Your greatness
    and Your nearness

Amen

July 16

A Thought

Jesus Christ is the same yesterday, today and for ever. The pre-existent Christ ('in the beginning was the Word') is Jesus of Nazareth who is 'my beloved Son', who died and rose again. The whole purpose of the 'Divine plan of salvation' is to restore humanity to the wholeness God seeks for all – which is one-ness with Himself, through Christ, in the Spirit. Integration is 'through the Spirit'.

A Prayer
When I am overwhelmed
  with darkness
    depression
    defeat
Lift my eyes
  my heart
    my soul
to the One 'lifted up' for me
Then may I be made new

Amen

July 17

A Thought
When Henry Drummond was unorthodox and theologically suspect, the great evangelist Sankey, whom he knew, asked where he stood. Drummond replied in memorable words, which he emphasised were *his* words and *his* deepest convictions: 'The power to set the heart right, to renew the springs of affection, comes from Christ. The sense of the infinite worth of a single soul, and the recoverableness of man at his worst are the gifts of Christ. The freedom from guilt, the forgiveness of sins, comes from Christ's Cross: the hope of immortality springs from Christ's grave...'

A Prayer
Come Holy Spirit, come
  cleanse me, so that I may be more holy
Fill me with new life
  breathe into me new power
And make my heart truly
  Your home

Amen

July 18

A Thought

Despite the violence and the vilification, the mobs and the murders, the robberies and the rapes, the wars and the rumours of wars, never let us forget the wonders of this amazing world – the beauty of the earth, the glories of the skies, the creative possibilities in the arts, science and technology, the gladness of children, the glory of so many people, the consistency of nature and the grace revealed, within the world, in Jesus. *How lovely* – despite so much – *is our dwelling-place!*

A Prayer
I stand before Your cross, O Lord, in wonder
"There was no other good enough,
to pay the price of sin"
Prevent me, O Lord, from
"crucifying You afresh"
Redeem me from that which
adds to Your pain
Then may I serve You only as You deserve

Amen

July 19

A Thought

Who is this Man that even the winds and sea obey Him? (Matthew 8:27). What is the origin of the 'authority' with which He speaks? The answer is in Peter's historic, intuitive summing-up of all that he had come to believe: 'Thou art the Christ, the Son of the living God' (Matthew 16:16).

Christ's 'mastery' is rooted in His divinity. 'You, call me Master and Lord... and so I am' (John 13:13). The Gospels therefore present Jesus as Master over disease, evil spirits and, ultimately, over death. It is in this capacity that He helps us.

A Prayer
O Master, let me walk
  in Your company
    hearing Your words
    seeing Your deeds
    feeling Your love
And having walked with You
  along the road of life
May I walk with others
  in Your name

Amen

July 20

A Thought

'Who will rescue me from this body which turns life into death?' asks Paul (Romans 7:24, William Barclay). The answer he gives himself (verse 25): 'God alone can through Jesus Christ our Lord. Thanks be to Him!'

A Prayer
Help me, O God
  to have
    a sense of humour
    a sense of fun
    an ability to laugh
  to use it
    never hurtfully
    always generously

Amen

July 21

A Thought

The secret of the life that is to be abundant is the reservoir of peace built into our wholeness; a reservoir that, if fed by the activity of the Divine Spirit, need never be exhausted.

A Prayer
Let the breath of the Spirit
  fall on me
Let the energy of the Spirit
  come into me
So may I be transformed and inspired
  to serve Your cause today

                              Amen

July 22

A Thought
We cannot move towards health or wholeness if we neglect the growth of the *spiritual* part of our beings. Any philosophy of life that fails to acknowledge this truth is, in the words of the old evangelical hymn, a 'broken cistern'. The salvation of the soul, the attainment of wholeness, integration – call it what you will – involves Christ at the centre and growth through the Spirit. This is the truth about life.

A Prayer
Let my love be without pretence
  May I abhor that which is evil
  Make me cleave to that which is good
All through the Christ who dwells within me

                              Amen

July 23

A Thought
If there is one passage in which the *New English Bible* translators have surpassed themselves, it must be the section Ephesians 3:14-21. There is hardly a word in it that does not lead to the things of the Spirit. Just take a part of it each day for a week and think on these words:
  'I kneel in prayer to the Father, from whom every family in heaven and on earth takes its name, that out of the treasures of his glory, he

may grant you strength and power through his Spirit in your inner being.'

The 'treasures of his glory'. 'Strength and Power'. 'Through his Spirit'. 'In your inner being'.

What a prayer!

A Prayer
  'Hallowed by Thy Name!'
  This loving reverence I offer
  in Jesus' name

                              Amen

July 24

A Thought

'That through faith, Christ may dwell in your hearts in love.' How central to Paul is 'faith', the soul's response to the gift of Christ. To be 'in Christ', to have Christ in you, is the goal of discipleship. It is possible – but by faith alone.

A Prayer
Help me, O Lord
  to know whom I have believed
  to be persuaded that You are able to do that
    which I have committed to You
Then shall I rest in peace
  knowing that it is not my grasp of You
  but Your grasp of me
  that is important

                              Amen

July 25

A Thought

'With deep roots...'

Roots, the growing tree, reaching heavenwards, but spreading its branches outwards too. It is so like the Christian personality – rooted in personal history and culture, growing heavenwards – towards Christ, reaching outwards – in community responsibility. So we become 'the leaves of the tree' that are for 'the healing of the nations'.

A Prayer
Make quiet my mind and heart
  for the inflow of God's Spirit
Illumine me with the Light of the world
Fill me with the Peace that passes all understanding
So there shall flow out of me to all
  Light and Peace and Love

Amen

July 26

A Thought
'...and firm foundations'. How rock-like it feels! How secure, Jesus said in the Sermon on the Mount, is 'the house built on rock'. How natural the Church should be built around Peter, 'the rock'. 'For other foundation can no man lay than that is laid, which is Jesus Christ' (1 Cor. 3:11). 'That Rock was Christ' (1 Cor. 10:4).

A firm foundation.

A Prayer
Lord, keep me safe this night
  secure from all my fears
May angels guard me while I sleep
  till morning light appears

Amen

July 27

A Thought
'With deep roots and firm foundations, may you be strong to grasp, with all God's people, what is the breadth, length, depth and height of

f Christ.' Salvation is the gift of God! We do not have to serve it, merit it, work for it. Just receive it! So let there be no tentative feeling-out: grasp it, take it, hold it, receive it. It is there – for all.

A Prayer
Amid life's storms, make me still
Amid life's changes, make me strong
If criticism comes, keep me steadfast
If sadness comes, keep me brave
  Make my weakness strong
  through the grace that is sufficient for me

Amen

July 28

A Thought

'Grasp the love of Christ and know it, though it is beyond knowledge.' What a paradox is in these words! A knowledge which is beyond knowledge! For the knowledge that comes in faith is another kind of knowledge. It is not subject to logic, rationality, proof. It is intuitional knowledge – or as Paul says to the Galatians, 'by direct revelation'.

We know Christ's love through that kind of knowledge.

A Prayer
Still the waves
Quieten the storms
Hold the tiller in your hand
Fill the sails with the wind of the Spirit
So may I reach the desired haven
And drop anchor in Your love

Amen

July 29

A Thought

'Now to Him who is able to do *immeasurably more* than all we can ask or conceive...' That phrase 'immeasurably more' sums up the vast difference between finite, human understanding and the infinite, Divine understanding. Our faith is not in the 'most' we can understand but in the 'more' of the Divine unlimitedness.

A Prayer
Grant to me, O Lord
Eyes to see the beauty of the world
and the inner eye to discern the wonder of the Spirit
Ears to hear the sounds of nature
and the inner ear to hear the music of the spheres
Hands to help me work and play and love
and hands of use to the Spirit for the healing of mankind

Amen

July 30

A Thought

'So may you attain to fullness of being, the fullness of God Himself.' The way to wholeness is through the way of Christ – in all its wonder. So faith alone is the way to fullness.

A Prayer
May the Light that shone in Christ, my Lord
illumine my heart
May that same Light
shine down the road that lies ahead of me
And suffuse my path with its radiance

Amen

July 31

A Thought

Apa Pant, the distinguished Indian writer and statesman, in his book *A Moment of Time*, tells of his 'journey of discovery', a journey for his soul. He says the journey would have been impossible but for the 'profound and powerful, constant and most loving, kind and at the same time challenging and demanding Presence that came to me as a privilege of life.'

A Prayer

Help me, O Lord, to see in moments of time, not merely coincidence, but the surprises of the Spirit
So may I live each day, conscious of Your Providence and aware of Your Presence in the significant 'moments of time', prepared for me Through Jesus Christ, our Lord

Amen

AUGUST

When all is dark...

August 1

A Thought

The text for the Divine Sensitivity is that 'He knows our needs before we ask.' The text for the Divine Empathy is that 'He suffered and was tempted... like as we are.'

A Prayer
Make me conscious, O Lord
  of the church militant of which I am a part
Make me conscious, O Lord
  of the church triumphant by which I am encompassed
May my awareness of
  the communion of Your saints be an encouragement to me
Through Jesus Christ, our Lord

Amen

August 2

A Thought

'Man's extremity is God's opportunity.' How true these words feel when I walk through the valley of the shadows. 'He descended into hell.' How real these words feel when I look at the depths from which people need lifting. But it is not 'man's extremity' that is decisive. It is the way God grasps the opportunity 'whereby we may be saved.'
For the God who acts so, let us give thanks.

A Prayer
All our hope is founded
  on You, O God
You forgive our iniquities
  You heal our diseases
  You crown us with loving-kindness and mercy

You redeem our lives from destruction
Our hope is surely placed

Amen

August 3

A Thought

There is no way to the healing of the memories that does not pass through the facing of the memories, the acknowledgement of the memories, the acceptance of the memories and the redemption of the memories. The road to resurrection goes via Calvary.

Per ardua ad astra is true in the life of the Spirit, too. It *is* through hurt and hardship we reach the stars.

A Prayer
Let remembrances of my failure, O Lord
  not be a wallowing in what I have failed to be and do
Let it rather lead me to
  the rock that is higher than I
  the grace which is all-sufficient
  the love that is all-forgiving
So may my failures be the
  place where victory begins

Amen

August 4

A Thought

'A weak faith,' writes Viktor Frankl (in *The Unconscious God)* 'is weakened by predicaments and catastrophes whereas a strong faith is strengthened by them.' The suffering saints have shown this again and again – to God's glory and our strengthening.

A Prayer
Send, O Lord
  Your ministering angels

silently, to enfold us
subtly, to strengthen us
sensitively, to encourage us
spontaneously, to surprise us
May the angels who came to minister to You, O Lord
  bring their blessings to Your people

Amen

August 5

A Thought
That well-known declaration by a young Jew on the wall of a Warsaw
ghetto never fails to move and stir:
  'I believe in the sun even if it does not shine
  I believe in love even though I do not feel it
  I believe in God even if I do not see Him.'

A Prayer
Bless us with friends, O Lord
  and bless them through us
Bless us when we have to stand alone
  and bear the pain only we can bear
Bless us through the Divine Friendship
  which comes when 'other helpers fail'
'O Thou who changest not
  Abide with me'

Amen

August 6

A Thought
Jesus' Gethsemane cry: 'Thy will, not mine be done' is about faith's
triumph over total disillusionment. The miracle of deliverance from
suffering, as Jesus knows, is not to happen, but the greater miracle of
resurrection is – and it did.

A Prayer
Keep me
  trusting in You, O God
  looking towards You, O Christ
  walking with You, O Holy Spirit
So may I have grace
  Thrice over

                    Amen

August 7

A Thought
There are many in the Garden of Gethsemane and we must pray for
them.

A Prayer
O Lord,
make me understanding
  of all that is around me
  accepting that which is good and lovely
  rejecting all that corrupts and destroys
  aware of all that you can redeem
both outside me and inside me

                    Amen

August 8

A Thought
We all have a right to our secrets, but to hold things back from God is
pointless, for (I repeat) 'He knows before we ask.' Do not hold back
honest recognition of your negative or 'shadow' side either. We need
to know and accept ourselves, 'warts and all', in order to make our
most creative contributions to life.

A Prayer
When I fail greatly
  lift me up
When I am arrogant
  put me down
When I love greatly
  give me joy
When I am loved greatly
  grant me peace
When love is taken away
  let me not be bitter
When love returns
  make me glad
When all seems lost
  support me
When all is well
  make me grateful

Amen

August 9

A Thought
Rejection, loneliness, desolation – all are parts of experience, and can feel like a load that is too heavy to be borne. But if the sense of rejection can be reduced and the sense of the never-rejecting God created; if loneliness can be lightened; if a tiny flower begins to bloom in the desert places, the day has not been in vain.

A Prayer
Make us conscious, O Lord
  of the infinite variety and diversity of Your world
   its cultures and its customs
   its many highways to truth
   its many ways of worship
And having seen such diversities of gifts

May we know
  the presence of one Holy Spirit
  the gift of one cosmic Christ who is the Son of the one God and
  Father of us all

Amen

August 10

A Thought

It is hard to believe "He holds the whole world in His hands' sometimes. War, violence, bombs, prejudice – the denial of His presence is so prevalent. But crucifixion precedes resurrection, while the hate of Calvary is the doorway to the resurrection of Love. The darkest hour *is* just before the dawn.

A Prayer
May I always know, O Lord, that all depends
  Not on my grasp of You
  But on Your grasp of me
Then will all be truly well

Amen

August 11

A Thought

We find it easy to quote Paul's words: 'All things work together for good' but often forget to complete the quotation which says 'to them that love God.' The qualification is important.

A Prayer
Grant, O Lord, that I may see Your hand
  in the way things work together for good
Grant, that, so seeing, I may want to
  love You more

And in the happenings of the Spirit
   may I see Your Love

Amen

August 12

A Thought

'Ought not Christ to have suffered these things?' asked the Stranger on the road to Emmaus. When those who are suffering deeply can see a shaft of light on the meaning of suffering that these words bring, the effect on 'total' health is remarkable. But it is only those who are in deep suffering who can pay tribute to such truth. On the lips of those for whom all seems to be going well, it sounds so glib.

A Prayer
How hard it is, O Lord
   to see You in the suffering
      of so many
But the suffering which was Yours
   has shed a light that illumines my way
   and so leads me to greater understanding
Bless that which I have learned through suffering

Amen

August 13

A Thought

I have twice learned, painfully, the danger of ignoring the inner pressure to do something. On both occasions, I did not go quickly enough to see two great churchmen, men of the Spirit, before they died in the prime of their lives. There was not time – but there ought to have been time, as I know now. Remembering George Gunn and Tom Allan, I try never to make that mistake of omission again. I do not know what they thought I could give them. I know what I missed.

A Prayer
O Lord, make me quick
  to hear
    to answer
      to minister
  make me aware of
    the smallest and most still voice within
      calling me to Your work

May I say with Samuel:
  'Speak. Lord, I hear'
    with Isaiah
      'Here am I, send me!'

                              Amen

August 14

A Thought

Carlo Carretto is well known as a profoundly spiritual soul. But he has as saints do (but are not always seen to have) a very practical side. He is helpful when he writes 'Don't keep saying "everything has collapsed already!" You will find it much more cheering and rewarding to think of yourself as building for a new tomorrow, than as defending a past already old.'

A Prayer
When everything is against me
  Grant me the will to strive
When everyone is against me
  Grant me the will to live
When all I have is threatened
  Grant me the strength to be

                              Amen

August 15

A Thought
Harry Williams in his book, *Tensions*, tells us that, in Jewish Rabbinic thought, man is said to have a Good Inclination and an Evil Inclination. In the Shema ('Thou shalt love the Lord thy God with all Thy heart', etc.) the Hebrew word for 'heart' occurs in the form spelt with two *beths,* so many rabbis interpreted this as indicating that man is to love God both with the Good *and* the Evil Inclination.
This is indeed an encouragement. Our most potential self-offering is in the 'redemption' of our negative or 'shadow' aspects.

A Prayer
Make me, O Lord
  slow to anger
  slow to provoke
Make me, too
  quick to reconsider
  quick to praise
  quick to make peace
So may I be a true minister of reconciliation

Amen

August 16

A Thought
Stricken, saddened, sorrowing humanity needs words of healing. Fortunately there are words that can redeem the agony of doubt, words that can intellectually meet the most profound thinking that can be done: words that can minister to the most disturbed emotions: words that can bring peace where there is no peace: words of assurance and reassurance: words of forgiveness and renewal; words of acceptance and achievement.
As Hosea said: 'Take with you words.'

A Prayer
O Word of God, incarnate
  let Your words of hope inspire me
  let Your words of peace comfort me
  let Your words of life renew me
  let Your words of love bless me
Through Him who is the Word

                                        Amen

August 17

A Thought
By the 'Divine Initiative', the offer of forgiveness comes and a right relationship to God is restored. God took that step in the Incarnation, Death and Resurrection of Christ. Forgiveness is dependent on nothing other than the acceptance of it. This is the heart of the Gospel.

A Prayer
May my love be expressed
  in adoration towards You
  in sacrifice for others
  in acceptance of myself
  in service to the world

                                        Amen

August 18

A Thought
'Crisis', in Chinese, is composed of two ideograms. One represents 'danger', the other 'opportunity'. This is indeed a symbolic reminder of the creative possibility of crisis. Crises are not usually pleasant, but, the nettle grasped, doors can open marvellously.

A Prayer
Look with Your searching eye at me, O God, and
  reveal to me my weaknesses
  clarify my uncertainties
So illumine my way, that the best I have to give
  may shine as a light in the world
Reflecting You, the Light of the world

                              Amen

August 19

A Thought

There is a corporate psychic 'negativity' within the life and soul of mankind that demands the redemptive activity of God at both conscious and unconscious levels, as much as the personal 'shadow' – our negative side – does. Forgiveness is the healing word where there is a healthy, realistic and appropriate guilt. Every act of worship must make real the 'blotting out' and renewal that is life redeeming. To the healthily guilty, 'let us worship God' is a declaration of assurance and peace.

A Prayer
Let me never wallow in my sin, Lord
  but only recognise that which separates me from Your love
  and offer it to You in faith
So may the blessing of relationship restored
  be the theme of all my praise

                              Amen

August 20

A Thought

'The followers of Christ are called by God,' says Thomas Merton (in *He is risen*), 'not according to their accomplishments, but according to His own purpose and grace.' This statement, Merton says, 'effectively disposes of a Christian inferiority complex which makes people think that because they never have amounted to anything in the eyes of others, they can never amount to anything in the eyes of God.'

A Prayer
May I spend this day, O God
  about Your business
    giving priority to the things of the
      Kingdom of Heaven
    finding perspective in the things
      of the kingdoms of this world
So may my balance be right
  and my day good

Amen

August 21

A Thought

It is the aim of 'the Tempter' from the beginning to the end of life to destroy 'the new creation' born of the presence of the Spirit. 'He' never lets up. Christ found this out in His own life, for the 'Satan' who left Jesus 'for a season' returned many times... not least in Gethsemane and at Calvary. The process of growth in grace is the arena where the cosmic war between good and evil is focussed in the soul of each individual.

A Prayer
Let me not fear, O Lord
  the 'powers of darkness in high places'
  for You are Lord of the universe
    Yours is the Power
Grant us the love that exorcises fear
Let Your love take over that love
  that it may be ever nearer 'perfect'

Amen

August 22

A Thought

The healing of the soul, the self, is so much more than the restitution of the body. Indeed the acceptance that physical healing cannot always be given may, in itself, be transformed into a ministry to the whole person. For those in the depths of pain, this is a hard saying: I say it however on the testimony of some who have suffered much.

A Prayer
Thanks be to You, O Lord
   for the witness of the good who suffer and therefore know
      Your presence
      Your redeeming grace
      Your transforming power
May their example be my inspiration

Amen

August 23

A Thought

What a subtle but profound thought is expressed by Jürgen Moltmann when he tells us that he had much to say at one time on 'the resurrection of the crucified Jesus' but that now he wants to dwell much more on 'the crucifixion of the risen Christ'. It is the suffering of the eternal God in Christ that means so much.

A Prayer
Nothing in my hand I bring, O God
I simply cling to Your cross
Naked, I come to You for dress
Helpless, I look to You for grace
Nor will I be left unblessed
Thank You for Your Love

Amen

August 24

A Thought

In human relationships, sensitivity is a requirement for any who seek to offer healing. It is a word that speaks of subtlety, sureness and sympathy. It is a concept that puts importance on empathy and intuition. Sensitivity is built on respect for personality, so will never seek to invade privacy, but it also has a prophetic quality that enables the healing agent to sense need, despair or guilt in advance.

A Prayer
When all forsook Your Son and fled, O God
  Would I have been strong?
When they denied Your Son, O God
  Could I have done otherwise?
When one betrayed Your Son, O Lord
  Might it not have been me?
I thank You, God
  that You know what is in man
    and in me
And still forgive, accept and redeem

                              Amen

August 25

A Thought

'The road to this freedom (the liberty of the Spirit) as to every other experience is God's grace and leads to Golgotha.' These words of Sister Eva of Friedenshort are true. The process is visible in the lives of the saints. But it is *so* hard to say it (because it is so easy to *say* it) to those who are undergoing exceptional suffering and cannot feel it to be true. Yet it is the constant testimony of those saintly folk who have suffered acutely over a long period, that it is the truth about life.

A Prayer
The day is past and over, Lord
  I have tried to give
    in loving care
      in compassion
        in prayer
May the gifts I have offered be to Your glory and for the good of those
  who have crossed my path
Now I am alone, abide with me
  For 'without Thee, I cannot live'
May Your grace be sufficient for me
  Always

Amen

August 26

A Thought
Should worship be peaceful or disturbing? Should preaching be comforting or challenging? Elijah brought such a prophetic word that they called him the 'troubler' of Israel. Jesus once said He came to bring, not peace, but a sword. So comfort or challenge? The answer must be 'both'. But the famous Scottish preacher, A. J. Gossip's demand that no sermon should be without comfort, tips the balance to that side.

A Prayer
When the circumstances of life separate me from those we would love
most
  Bless me with the divine closeness
Help me accept courageously but graciously
  all that prevents commitment and self giving
Then may I be enabled to offer my pent-up love
  in the service of mankind

Amen

August 27

A Thought

Jesus said: 'Go ye into all the world.' That is indeed a challenge! But He also used the 'comfortable' words: 'Come unto me, all ye that labour and are heavy-laden, and I will give you rest.'

The balance remains tipped to the side of comfort. We cannot really challenge the world while we are 'weary and heavy-laden'. So first, rest in the Lord, then truly say: 'Here am I, send me.'

A Prayer
When I feel the loneliness of life
  be a very present help, O Lord
When I feel the frustrations of life
  make me still, O Lord
When I become depressed about life
  lift up my eyes and heart, O Lord
When I lose control of life
  make me a captive, Lord
And so help me regain my true freedom
                              Amen

August 28

A Thought

There are many devotional classics but in any list these four will surely have a place: Augustine's *Confessions,* Thomas à Kempis' *Imitation of Christ,* John Bunyan's *Pilgrim's Progress* and Henry Drummond's *The Greatest Thing in the World.*

A Prayer
0 Lord
  may I leave aside that which is grace-less
  may I love all that is grace-full

> *may I live graciously*
> *And so, grace-filled*
> *may I be an instrument of Your Peace*
>
> > *Amen*

August 29

A Thought

'All these things are against me' as Jacob said over the loss of his sons. This is the story of life for some. Why does it happen to me? they say. Or does it happen to me partly at least because I am 'me'? If the answer to the latter question is in the affirmative, it is time for us to ask questions about ourselves.

A Prayer
Give me, O Lord
  unlimited patience
  unlimited understanding
  unlimited love
Then I will be able to forgive
  as 1 have been forgiven
to bless
  as I have been blessed

> *Amen*

August 30

A Thought

The Gospel is not a Gospel of dis-couragement, but of en-couragement, and no preacher dare forget that fact. Jesus came not to condemn the world, but to save it.

A Prayer
Teach me the discipline, Lord
that is within
So may my inner strength be secured
and my heart be at peace
Teach me the discipline, O Lord
that comes from You
So may my life be lived
within Your grasp of me

Amen

August 31

A Thought

It is a long time since John Baillie's *A Diary of Private Prayer* was published, but the prayers in it are, fundamentally, timeless. Like this, for example:

For the power Thou has given me
to lay hold of things unseen
For the strong sense I have that
this is not my home
For my restless heart, which nothing
finite can satisfy,
I give Thee thanks, O God

A Prayer
Help me with pain, Lord
the physical pain in my body
the emotional pain in my heart
the spiritual pain in my soul
the pain of my mind
If, in my weakness, I must bear it
Make me to know Your strength is with me too

Through Jesus Christ, our Lord Amen

SEPTEMBER

I triumph still!

September 1

A Thought

'Jesus came, the doors being shut.' But is not that, miraculously now as it was then, exactly then when we feel His presence?

A Prayer

Give me a sense of adventure, O Lord
So that I may dream dreams and see visions
So work in me that I make them into realities
that bring blessings
Grant me
Deepened awareness
so that I do not merely dream
Heightened intuition
so that I am not limited by logic
Acute perception
so that I am able to calculate risks correctly
Through Jesus Christ, our Lord Amen

September 2

A Thought

Always, in times of pain, there is, somewhere, a rainbow.

A Prayer

Grant me O Lord the courage
to climb the rainbow through the rain
to feel the promise is not vain
to know the eternal truth again –
The Lord is risen!
Amen

September 3

A Thought
'My will is not mine own
   till Thou has made it Thine;
If it would reach a monarch's throne
   it must its crown resign.'

So George Matheson encapsulates the paradox that is, in human terms, foolishness, in divine terms, faith triumphant. The only way to growth is through death. The only way to resurrection is the way of the Cross. The only way to victory is through surrender.
And from the ground there blossoms red
Life that shall endless be.

A Prayer
It is not easy, willingly, O Lord
   to follow Your way
But I will, with grace abounding,
   give of myself to You
   trying to do Your will
   trying to give and not count the cost
   trying to be obedient at all times
When I fail, forgive
At all times, bless

                              Amen

September 4

A Thought
Spring will come. The great principle is true – both in nature and in the life of the Spirit. After death, there is new life. After the darkness there comes the dawn. After the Cross, and the descent into hell, there is, always, Resurrection.

A Prayer
When I pass through the valley of the shadows
  Keep my hope alive
    my faith real
    my peace intact
Then when the light at the end of the valley shows,
  Make me truly glad

                    Amen

September 5

A Thought
The desert, in the language of prayer, is the place of both desolation and encounter with God. May times of desolation become times of encounter, because our 'extremity' is indeed God's opportunity.

A Prayer
At dawn,
  grant me expectation
In the morning
  make me diligent
As the day goes on
  increase my serenity
Towards evening
  help me towards tranquillity
At the end of the day
  give me peace

                    Amen

September 6

A Thought
The drab and dreary vision of the Valley of Dry Bones in Ezekiel is not really about death. It is about resurrection, restoration and life. The Word, the Spirit and living in relationship with God are

all factors in that resurrection – according to Ezekiel; or rather God through Ezekiel.

A Prayer
Give me life, O Lord
  through the healing of my body
            the healing of my memories
            the healing of my emotions
            the healing of my mind and
            the healing of my soul

                              Amen

September 7

A Thought
The Gospel record is full of the sensitivity of Christ. 'Sheep without a shepherd' caught His attention even though He had retired to quietness. Children and parents, rebuked by the disciples, heard Him saying: 'Suffer the little children to come unto Me, and forbid them not.' The key... His sensitivity to need, the knowledge He had of the human condition, His ability to empathise with the sufferer, His insight into the workings of the human heart. Sensitivity lies at the very heart of God. He understands. He loves.

A Prayer
May I ever be a channel of blessing, Lord
  to the lonely
    to the distressed
      to the despairing
May I give of my hope
  my faith
    my love
  without thought of return

                              Amen

September 8

A Thought

Cardinal Suesens, the Roman Catholic writer, who played such a part in Vatican II writes profoundly on hope in his *Ways of the Spirit*:

'Reflect upon winter in the woods. Trees which seem to be devoid of life are waiting for the sap to rise. Lopped branches enable others to take their place. Winter is not an end: it is a soil wherein the foliage of the future is nurtured. Winter is not desolation: it is a time of waiting. It is darkness before the dawn.'

A Prayer
Looking unto Jesus, may I ever see
 Life
  Abundant
   Creative
    Eternal
And know that, through Him alone
 that life is given to me

       Amen

September 9

A Thought

It is hard to accept the pain of growth, for growing-pains are part of the evolving life of the Spirit. It is hard to reject 'the flesh' in favour of 'the spirit' and many a time in life great sorrow and bitter tears may wash our refusal to meet that demand. But the very confrontation we have had with reality, in all its stark sorrow or terrible tragedy may be *the ground of our becoming,* the soil in which new life is nurtured, the dismal death that leads to glorious resurrection.

A Prayer
I thank You, Lord
   that You did descend into hell
For You showed You save
   to the uttermost
That Your love reaches to the
   lowest depths of human darkness
May the memory of Your descent
   make my prayers the more ascend to You

                          Amen

September 10

A Thought

Consistency is an attribute of God as the Old Testament emphasises again and again. God does not change. God does not react on the basis of whim. He is the God of Abraham, Isaac and Jacob and equally the God of David, John the Baptist, Paul and Christ.

For the Divine consistency expressed throughout the life of the Son of Man who is Son of God, we ought to be eternally grateful.

'O Thou who changest not, abide with me.'

A Prayer
Guard me
   Guide me
      Keep me
         Feed me
For I have no help but Yours, O God
But with that help, all things are possible to me

                          Amen

September 11

A Thought

Love has an ability to take adverse circumstances and see in them the opportunity for spiritual growth. It is just that. To bear and to endure, in terms of Love, means taking, and accepting, grasping whatever is to our hurt and redeeming it so that it becomes a spiritually beneficial experience. *Nothing* need remain 'negative' when the Spirit is present.

A Prayer
I bind unto myself, O God
  the strong name of the Trinity
    Rejoicing in Your Fatherhood
    Glorying in Jesus our Lord
    Growing in the Spirit
So may I know
  Three blessings in one

                    Amen

September 12

A Thought

There is a road that leads, so they say, from the very gates of heaven towards hell. Maybe. But, more important, there is a road that leads from the very gates of hell back towards heaven. Christ, who descended into hell, made sure of this for us.

A Prayer
May I draw on the resources that are within
And through courage, determination and willpower go on,
  O Lord
May I draw even more on the resources that are in You
I will then do all things through Christ, who strengtheneth me

                    Amen

September 13

A Thought

It is often a matter of agonising guilt if failure continues after a profound spiritual experience. It shouldn't happen again, we feel. But it does. And it will.

It may help to recall the timing of Christ's temptation crisis. It follows *immediately after* the declaration, at the descent of the Spirit, that He is God's 'beloved Son' in whom He was well-pleased.

A Prayer
'When I survey the wondrous Cross'
  give me
    penitence
      assurance
        humility
And let me not put my trust
  in anything but the grace You give

                    Amen

September 14

A Thought

God's demand to Elijah to forget about earthquakes, wind, fire and other natural circumstances as well as to put behind him his inner conflicts and suicidal inclinations, and simply listen to 'the still, small voice' of Divine reality is a demand made to us all. It is a loving command made to us to *stop amid listen!*

A Prayer
Watch with me, O God
  in temptation
  in pain
    in gloom

And by Your presence
  safeguard me
    comfort me
      uphold me

                    Amen

September 15

A Thought
The man or woman ready for God's service is the one who has seen and recognised the secret self and has come to creative terms with it.
It is no surprise that the truly human Jesus faced His own 'other' ('shadow') side in the temptations, as subtle and powerful temptations as 'Satan' could devise, for they concentrated on the possibility that Christ might, in His own interest, abuse His divine power.
That divine power which Jesus would not abuse became in fact the very power through which He could fulfil His mission.
The facing of our secret self can similarly become our strength.

A Prayer
Wherever I walk, O Lord
  may my light shine
      my love radiate
      my grace grow
      my peace bless
And so may others feel the presence of my Lord

                    Amen

September 16

A Thought
'It is more humanly beautiful to risk failure' writes Mark Gibbard in his *Guide to Hidden Springs*, 'searching for the hidden springs than to resign to the futurelessness of the wasteland. For the springs are there to be found.'

A Prayer
Lead me, O Lord
  by still waters
And so
  restore my soul
Guide me, O Lord
  through Your still, small voice
And so
  renew my confidence
Walk with me, O Lord
  in the stillness and
    reassure me of Your nearness

                    Amen

September 17

A Thought

'God was in Christ, reconciling the world to Himself.' Christ must be in us, compelling us to see that if our broken relationships are to be healed, we have no alternative but to take that first step towards reconciliation. The possibilities that will open up when that move is finally, even if reluctantly, made may well be the nearest things to miracles that we shall see in life.

A Prayer
The day You have given, O Lord
  is ending and
The darkness falls at Your behest
May our morning hymns have ascended
  to praise You
May You now sanctify our rest

                    Amen

September 18

A Thought

Spiritual exploration, like other forms of exploration, demands both risk and responsibility. Responsibility is needed otherwise we may be seduced and jump on any contemporary bandwagon; risk because there is a call to 'launch out into the deep' in Christianity.

'Abraham went out – not knowing whither he went.' But look what followed!

Take risks – for the sake of Christ and His cause.

A Prayer
To risk myself, my future
  for You, O God
is to ask too much, too often
Yet without risk
  Your cause is stifled
  Without adventure
  Your work remains undone
Give me, O God, the grace
  to 'take a chance' for You

Amen

September 19

A Thought

  Do you know Christopher Logue's words?
  'Come to the edge' –
  It's too high
    'Come to the edge'
  We might fall
    'Come to the edge'
  And they did...
  And they flew!

A Prayer
May I, if You so call me
  be proud to be a fool for Christ's sake
May I undertake the humanly impossible
  in faith
May I accept the risks
  in trust
May I respond to the call to
  Divine adventure

                    Amen

September 20

A Thought

Responsibility is perhaps response-ability. It means making a response to a need, a situation, a challenge. The disciples showed response-ability. So did John Wilberforce, David Livingstone, George Fox, Martin Luther King, Alida Bosshardt, Mother Teresa and how many more? The dramatic irony of the situation is that having taken response-ability, they then showed 'creative irresponsibility', that is undertaking enterprises no 'responsible' person would and creating marvels by doing so!

A Prayer
What shall I render to You, O Lord
  for all Your benefits to me?
Give me a thankful heart
        a willing body
        a sharp and clear mind
        a dedicated soul

                    Amen

September 21

A Thought
The phrase 'ministry of encouragement' is worth thought. The church must be a 'community of encouragement' for after all Jesus came (He said) not to condemn, but to save. Why do we so often discourage people by criticism, by judgemental attitudes? Comfort, acceptance, support – against such concepts there is no law.

A Prayer
Make me a captive, Lord
  so may I find true freedom
Make me 'poor in spirit' Lord
  so may I find true richness
Make me lowly of heart, Lord
  so may I feel true rest in my soul

                              Amen

September 22

A Thought
David, we are told, in a crisis 'encouraged himself in the Lord, his God'. Encouraged himself! There is a village in the north of England called 'Pity Me'. How often we make our home there! Self-pity is humanly understandable but is of no constructive help. We must fight and fight and fight again, said Hugh Gaitskell in a famous rallying call. So must we all, even when everything seems against us.
Encourage yourself!

A Prayer
Breathe on me, breath of God
  Fill me with life anew
That 1 may love what Thou dost love
  And do what Thou wouldst do

                              Amen

September 23

A Thought

How does one encourage oneself in the Lord our God? By recalling the things about God that are reassuring. He is always the same – yesterday, today and for ever. He is utterly consistent. He makes things work together for good. He is infinite in forgiveness, loving-kindness and tender mercy. He is Love.

What encouragement!

A Prayer
Purge me and make me clean, O Lord
   Create a new heart within me
      And a right spirit
Spirit Divine, attend my birth into new life
   And make my body, heart, mind and soul together
      Your temple and Your home

                              Amen

September 24

A Thought

To see age in action is always encouraging. Emmanuel Shinwell addressing the Labour Party Conference in his nineties, Dr Winifred Rushforth of Edinburgh developing Encounter Groups at 92, an organist – anonymous – enthusing over a new electronic instrument in his mid-eighties, having cycled to church! This is indeed a ministry of encouragement to us all!

A Prayer
May I so live that, in the daily race
   the things of God may hold the highest place

From that perspective, may I seek
  not glory
      or thanks
        or credit
But find my reward in the knowledge
  that I have tried to do Your will

Amen

September 25

A Thought

It is always a privilege to sense a saint of God in a congregation, but there he was – mid-eighties, alert, singing the songs of love with fervour and conviction; triumphant still from the time when, in the trenches in the First World War, he saw Christ beside him and heard His word of assurance, just before he had to go 'over the top' ('It all turned out just as He said,'), to the present time of separation from his wife through death. What a witness to the Faith!

A Prayer
Walk with me
  through the darkness, O Lord
Stay beside me through the shadows
Go ahead of me across the rocky way
Support me in the turbulent flood
So may I feel always in Your company

Amen

September 26

A Thought

The test of 'the community of encouragement' – which the church must be – is its ability to be supportive when the situation is a difficult one. The ministry of encouragement is not about bonhomie of a superficial kind. It is about the ability to act supportively when things go seriously wrong. It is about non-judgemental acceptance of situations that may be threatening to its peace and welfare. It is about standing by the member who has publicly failed and ensuring that, instead of bringing him down and casting him out, he or she will be held within the family and drawn upwards – encouraged – by the community of grace.

A Prayer
Make me a force for good, O Lord
   so that, in the intense conflict between good and evil
   I may contribute to that which is of You
      and combat all that is foreign to Your will

                    Amen

September 27

A Thought
Life, Peter Ustinov has commented, is coming to realise all the things you cannot do. The moral is that we must develop any skill we have and, finding that we have the potential to do something creative, go on and do it whatever happens. There is no limit to our unused potential and no matter what our age is, we must use all of it that we can.

A Prayer
   Here we seek no abiding city
   we seek one to come
I press toward the mark
   for the prize of the high calling of God in Christ Jesus
Lord, nudge us ever forward, onward, outward, upward

                    Amen

September 28

A Thought
'The dreamers are the saviours of the world.' So wrote James Allen in
As a Man Thinketh. It sounds romantic and idealistic, but Allen is
right. 'The greatest achievements were at first and for a time dreams.'

A Prayer
In my convictions
* make me firm*
In my judgements
* make me sensitive*
In my efforts to speak truth
* anchor me in love*
And when I am criticised
* let me not be bitter*
*   but follow rather the example of Christ, my Lord*
Amen

September 29

A Thought
The sort of person Zacchaeus was – or had become – certainly assured
him of power, but it deprived him of popularity. Detested for what he
did and, in due course, for all he was, he became a lonely man, small
in stature, but small in self-value too. Zacchaeus had neither inner
strength nor friends to support him, so he was, naturally, interested in
the man of whom he had heard so much good. He wanted to see
'what Jesus looked like'. It was the desire to look at Jesus that took
him tree-climbing.

A Prayer
I praise You, O God
* from the heights of my joy*
*   and in the depths of my grief, sorrow and pain*

I praise You, O God
  that You rejoice if I rejoice
    and weep when I weep
I thank You for the smile You bring to me
  and the tears You wipe away
I praise You O God
  I acknowledge You to be my Lord

Amen

September 30

A Thought

There are walls and barriers that men create to try to stifle contact and conversation, but they only succeed in part. Dietrich Bonhoeffer was put to death, but he still speaks to the world. Christ was crucified in an effort to stop His message and His influence. But near 2,000 years later, it is still proclaimed.

Yes, indeed, whatever people do, 'the Lord reigneth.'

A Prayer
Make me an agent of reconciliation
  so that
    where division reigns
    where communication ceases
    where love has gone
  I draw people together
    with cords of love
So may they be bound together
  through Him to whom I am bound
Even Jesus Christ, our Lord

Amen

OCTOBER

The Spirit and the Silence

October 1

A Thought

'The Healing of the Memories' is a phrase of great beauty and profundity. I see it as a process involving the activity of the Spirit, not only within our conscious understanding, but deep in the hidden places psychology calls the 'unconscious'. It has to do with realisation, acceptance, forgiveness and transformation. In other words with 'integration through the Spirit'.

A Prayer
In times of pressure
  grant me peace
In times of harassment
  grant me hope
In times of stress
  grant me serenity
In times of sadness
  grant me strength
At all times offer me
  Your benediction

Through Jesus Christ, our Lord, Amen

October 2

A Thought

Cardinal Suesens, the Roman Catholic writer I have already quoted, said at Pentecost, 1974: 'I believe in the surprises of the Holy Spirit.'

There are indeed many of them, if we have the eyes of faith.

A Prayer
Grant me
  the sense of wonder that says:

'Speak Lord, I hear'
the sense of repentance that pleads:
'Wash me... and I shall be clean'
the sense of gladness that shouts:
'He makes all things new'
Thus may I be truly a new creation

Amen

October 3

A Thought

Metropolitan Ignatias offered these words on the Holy Spirit at a World Council of Churches meeting in 1968.

'Without the Holy Spirit
God is far away
Christ stays in the past
the Gospel is simply an organisation
authority a matter of propaganda
the liturgy is no more than an evolution
Christian loving, a slave morality.'

A Prayer
Touch me
* with Your Spirit*
Embrace me
* in Your Love*
Enfold me
* in Your Peace*
Uphold me
* in Your Strength*

Amen

October 4

A Thought

Metropolitan Ignatias goes on:

'But in the Holy Spirit
the cosmos is resurrected and grows
with the birth pangs of the Kingdom
the Risen Christ is there
the Gospel is the power of life
the Church shows forth the life of the Trinity
authority is a liberating service
mission is a Pentecost
the liturgy is both renewal and anticipation
human action is deified.'

A Prayer
'Come, holy Dove
expand Thy wings
the wings of peaceful love'
Make me conscious of
the protection of the Spirit
the cleansing of the Spirit
renewal by the Spirit
Breathe on me, breath of God
Fill me with life anew

Amen

October 5

A Thought

Who... or what... would control the life of Christ?

That was the battle He fought in the desert.

To whom would Paul belong and whom must he serve?

These were the issues he faced in the desert of Arabia.

How shall we find the way to integration and wholeness?

That is the question we take to the stillness of our desert, wherever it may be.

The answer we shall discover, as Paul did, in partnership with the Spirit.

A Prayer
Make me a medium of Your peace
  to the anxious, frightened, frustrated, lonely and distressed
May the peace 'which passes understanding' be found
  in the caring I convey and
  in the serenity I share

                          Amen

October 6

A Thought
Dependence on the Holy Spirit is sometimes made an excuse for doing no homework before speaking, but the Holy Spirit cannot, of course, work on nothing. It is the well-stored, disciplined mind that is the vehicle of the Spirit.

A Prayer
Grant me the word of grace
  to troubled souls
Let me show the act of grace
  to unhappy lives
Make me living grace
  to all with whom I have to do

                          Amen

October 7

A Thought
There is a ministry of silence in the Christian faith. One element in it is the need for silence about others. St Paul said on sensationalism and gossip: 'Love is not glad when things go wrong; love rejoices in the truth.' If we cannot speak well of people, perhaps we are called to keep silence about them.

A Prayer
Let me no more my comfort draw

From my frail hold of Thee
In this alone rejoice with awe
  Thy mighty grasp of me
So may I feel the everlasting arms beneath me

Amen

October 8

A Thought

There is a place for silence in prayer. It is the time when the asking stops and the listening begins: a time when there is a genuine 'waiting on the Lord' and a receptiveness to His presence. That is the time when the Spirit comes.

A Prayer
In the silence
  I adore
In the silence
  I repent
In the silence
  I give thanks
In the silence
  I pray
But in the silence, too
  I listen
'Speak, Lord, for Thy servant heareth'

Amen

October 9

A Thought

So much of prayer is words addressed to God – and properly so. We must voice our praises, our thanks, our confessions, our dedication. But in any relationship there must be conversation, not monologue. In other words in our relationship with God, He too must speak, and we must in silence – listen.

A Prayer
Give me an understanding of what I do to others
  an appreciation of what others do for me
Give me respect for another's personality and freedom
  So that I do not force on them
    my care-full anxiety or
    my care-less words
May I then offer more, not less
  but always at the right time

Amen

October 10

A Thought
A striking element in the ministry of silence is the silence of dignity, that silence displayed by our Lord when blasphemous questions were thrown at Him by His accusers. 'He answered them nothing.'
There are times when the only answer to the things people say is dignified silence.

A Prayer
May I live each day with respect
  For all that is good in the past
  With understanding of all that is part of the present
  With enthusiasm for all that is now in the future
In the company of Him who is the same yesterday, today and for ever

Amen

October 11

A Thought
A silence that must be recovered is the silence of awe and wonder, the reaction so often displayed in biblical times in the presence of God. Respect is not a contemporary characteristic – whether it be for property, old age, relationships of intimacy or even God.

  The recovery of the silence of awe before the One who is holy and

who has shown His love in Christ, is a priority. It must begin within
the church itself.

A Prayer
For the unity we have
  We thank You, O God
For the unity not yet possible
  We ask the power to search
Restore the shattered Cross
  through the Power of Your Spirit
And gather, in Your own good time
  all Christians in true communion

                              Amen

October 12

A Thought
More is often said by silence than by sounds. Think of that moment of
silent wonder in the presence of holy beauty... Think of the effect of a
period of silence in worship, music or meditation... Think how much
more is said by silent loving embrace in bereavement than halting,
hesitant words, however sincere, can say... Think of the silences of
love...
'Be still...'

A Prayer
Help me to look at everything around me, O God
  and find reason for Praise
Help me to listen to the sounds of nature, O God
  and find reason to give Thanks
Help me notice the signs of need, O God
  and be ready to respond
Help me to feel the pain of all, O God
  and be there to help with love

                              Amen

October 13

A Thought

Hold to the silence of wonder! It is the *awe-full* silence that human beings should feel in the presence of the holy; the silence the numinous compels: the silence of speechlessness that recognition of the divine dimension demands.

It is a silence our over-sophisticated society and perhaps even our churches need to know.

A Prayer
Make me like salt, O Lord
  so that, retaining 'the savour' through grace
    I may feed society with love
    I may stimulate society to life
    I may encourage society by example

                    Amen

October 14

A Thought

It is essentially human to retaliate when accusations are made against us. It may even be right to do so on occasions. But there is, in Christ's example (see October 10), a reminder of the power of the silence of conviction, the silence of assurance that comes from a heart that remains unaffected and untouched by trivial taunts and heartless hate. This is the silence of dignity shown by Jesus when, in response to His accusers, He answered nothing.

A Prayer
May the holiness I seek, O Lord
  be the holiness I find in You
May the grace I convey, O Lord
  be the grace that is from You
May the hope I offer, O Lord
  be the hope that is in You
May the life that I live, O Lord
be the life You live in me

                    Amen

October 15

A Thought

Wendy Robinson (in *Exploring Silence*) talks of four 'shapes of silence': The Silence of Availability (necessary passivity); The Silence of Growth (the silence of gestation); Silence beyond Words (pure silence – after words, the silence of lovers) and The Silence of the Pieta (the silence of suffering and the mystery of death). These are indeed silences to be explored – with Wendy (see Book References).

A Prayer
How wonderful, O God
  is the Divine humility
You washed feet
  You had no place to lay Your head
    You became obedient unto death
      despising its shame
Let Your humility invade me
  so that I be no more
    proud and arrogant
      self-laudatory and loud
but reflect Your humility

Amen

October 16

A Thought

The Christian community will bless the world if it can do anything to contribute to the restoration of silence as a therapeutic component in the healing of mankind.

A Prayer
Give mine the ability to be still
  so that my stillness will help others
Give me the quality of peace
  so that my inner calm will calm others

Give me the attitude of compassion
  so that I am found to be caring
Give mine the characteristics of Christ
  so that I may bring blessings in His name

                                    Amen

October 17

A Thought
'There is such a thin line between tears and laughter' a letter-writer says. And between love and hate. And between anger and reconciliation. The presence of the Spirit is so necessary when we balance on these lines – to nudge us to the right side.

A Prayer
When we walk through
  a vale of tears
    take our hands, O Lord
When we dance over
  a mountain of laughter
    clap Your hands, O Lord
When we stand in the
  valley of decision
    take our arm, O Lord
And let us know that, always
  those everlasting arms are underneath

                                    Amen

October 18

A Thought
Too often we expect miracles from heaven and forget the need to 'prepare the way of the Lord'. To plan for the Spirit is not to deny His power, but to acknowledge it.

A Prayer
I wait on You, O God
  in reverence
    in humility
      in penitence
        in trust
May the finitude of my expectation
  be swamped in the infinity of Your grace
So waiting, may I be filled

Amen

October 19

A Thought
Grace is a gift and grace brings growth. It is a gift nothing we can do can earn. It brings growth for it is the energy of the Spirit promised by Christ. Grace is therefore 'sufficient' for us.

There is no higher gift than 'grace'.

A Prayer
Pour out Your Spirit on me
O Lord
May I learn the vibrations
of that Spirit
May I feel the energy
of that Spirit
So that I may pour out on others
the gift that has been given to me

Amen

October 20

A Thought
In every part of life, one principle holds true. We cannot 'give out' if we do not 'take in'.

Without the falling rain, the reservoirs diminish. Without the gentle

breeze the windmill stays motionless. Without the gift of water from the sky, the rivers fail and the mountain streams dry up. Without taking in breath, there is no hope in life. Without the appropriate amount of food, strength goes. Without sleep, we have no energy.
It is the same in the life of the Spirit.

A Prayer
Grant me, O God
  the generosity to give
    without counting the cost to me
  the grace to receive
    without counting the cost to others
Then shall I know the Joy both giving and receiving
  gratefully
  graciously

                    Amen

October 21

A Thought
'I will lift up mine eyes to the hills. From whence cometh my help? My help cometh from the Lord.'

While saints have been found in the city, they have tended to nourish their souls on the hills or in the desert; near the earth; often in solitude. Jesus was crucified in or around the city. The strength He needed to face it, He found on the hillside, or in a garden.

A Prayer
May the 'still dews of quietness'
  drop around me and on me
So stilled, may I radiate peace
  everywhere
And widen the area of serenity

                    Amen

October 22

A Thought

I paraphrase some very important words of Paul in Philippians 4:11-12. 'In every situation I have been in,' says Paul (and he gives a list of very traumatic situations) 'I have found a creative opportunity. I have, within the limits of any given set of circumstances however intolerable, found a way to use those circumstances positively. And so, while accepting these limitations as reality – as "the things that cannot be changed" – I have found in and through them true contentment.'

Limitation, hostility and adversity are, spiritually speaking, learning situations. They develop our resources, so increasing our faith and evolving our maturity. As the *New English Bible* puts it: 'I have learned to find resources in myself whatever the circumstances.'

A Prayer
O God grant me
  strength of body
    so that I may be creative for Your Kingdom
  strength of mind
    so that I may think clearly about Your Kingdom
  strength of will
    so that I may discipline myself for the Kingdom
  strength of faith and
    so that I may believe in the things of the Kingdom

                    Amen

October 23

A Thought

'Try the spirits,' we are told, 'to see if they are of God.' Here is the test. Good spirits console and fortify. Evil spirits afflict, agitate and depress.

A Prayer
The Lord bless you and keep you
The Lord make His face to shine upon you
*   and be gracious unto you*
The Lord lift up His countenance upon you
*   and give you peace*

Amen

October 24

A Thought

The Holy Spirit produces, not disorder but order. That is an important guideline in making any assessment of manifestations claimed to be of 'the Spirit'.

A Prayer
Grant, O Lord that
*   Forgetting the things which are behind*
*   I may reach forward energetically*
*   Remembering the things which are behind*
*   I may' the more 'press toward the mark'*
*   for the prize of the high calling of God in Christ Jesus*
So may I learn of Your purpose
*   and follow Your path*

Amen

October 25

A Thought

St Ignatius Loyola, we are told, found that daydreams of his own glory, while pleasant at the time, left him tired, bored and sad, while his dreams of being a second St Francis left him content and joyful. Thus he found he was sifting his emotions and beginning to see clearly which were the promptings of the Spirit. This he later called 'Discernment of Spirits'.

A Prayer
Make me aware, O God
  when it is Your voice I hear
Then will I do Your will
  and follow Your Way
Help me always
  to test the spirits
  to see what is of God and
  to embrace these

                    Amen

October 26

A Thought
The late John Baillie who wrote (among other things) *Invitation to Pilgrimage* and *A Diary of Private Prayer,* tells us there never was a time when he was not aware of God. He was brought up 'within' the faith.

Sometimes we put great stress – and not without reason – on a dramatic conversion, but steady growth in grace, ending in public commitment, is genuine, too.

A Prayer
May I, O Lord, be
  sure and steadfast
My anchor dropped deeply
  in Your love
So may I reach the desired haven

                    Amen

October 27

A Thought
Mother Mary Clare has a word for us in times when prayer is difficult. She says: 'Prayer is not conditioned by clock-time. It is a total

relationship with God that enables us to move easily from the day to day demands of life into a loving familiarity with God.'

A Prayer
Help me to find
  time to encourage
  time to forgive
  time to be still
  time to rise up
Let me never allow my time
  to be so full that I cannot serve

Amen

October 28

A Thought
The search for Truth is like climbing a mountain. We all start from different bases. We cannot see each other, so we do not know who is on the way or where. Truth is found only when we reach the top for there everything is in perspective.

We are all climbers, moving towards truth, but we come to it from different directions.

The main thing is to Keep Climbing!

A Prayer
I ask not to see
I ask not to know
  I ask only to be used

(A prayer of Cardinal Newman)

October 29

A Thought
  'What is that to thee? Follow thou me!'
These sharp words to Peter at the end of St John's Gospel constitute

the call to obedience Jesus issued regularly. The call involves total commitment, leaving other people's affairs out of our reckoning, and being nonconformist if necessary.

It is not easy to be 'different'. It may nevertheless be a demand we have to meet in Christian discipleship, helped by the Spirit.

A Prayer
O God, make it my concern
　to seek first Your Kingdom and its righteousness
　leaving other things to look after themselves
　to love You with heart and soul and mind and strength
　and my neighbour as myself
　to bear all things
　believe all things
　hope all things
So may my balance be right
　and my perspective clear

Amen

October 30

A Thought
If you are worried because you feel you have committed the so-called 'sin against the Holy Spirit', then you need worry no more. The point about that sin is that you simply do not have the capacity to worry about it. So hardened is the heart that a state is reached where there is total inability to distinguish evil from good. Those who called Jesus 'Beelzebub' had nearly reached that most dangerous spiritual condition. When you do not see any difference between Jesus and Satan, then it is time to worry about being almost beyond forgiveness. For forgiveness is a response to repentance. If the capacity for repentance has gone, how can forgiveness come?

A Prayer
Forgive, O Lord, my foolish ways
  my lustful heart
  my ill-tempered attitude
  my envy
  my disregard of others
And change these foolish ways
  to better things

                    Amen

October 31

A Thought

There are times when we *are* called to nonconformity! Faith triumphant may even involve being 'a fool for Christ's sake'.

Thoreau wrote: 'If a man does not keep pace with his companions, perhaps it is because he hears a different drummer. Let him step to the music he hears, however measured and far away...'

A Prayer
Give me the strength
              courage
                    faith
    to be different
      separated
        a fool for Christ's sake
If this be Your will
May I then stand and withstand
  for Your sake

        Through Jesus Christ, our Lord Amen

NOVEMBER

Healing Power

November 1

A Thought

The search for 'the healing of the memories' ends at the table of the Lord, for there the source of grace and the experience of grace is made real.

The Sacrament is not merely a memorial. It is a *means* of grace. *There* is the memory that heals. 'This do in remembrance of me.' 'You must continue to do this to make you remember me' (William Barclay).

A Prayer
You came, O Lord,
  sweet influence to impart
I thank You for the influence
  that surrounded me through others' faith
  the influence that comes through Word and Sacrament
  the influence I feel through the community of grace
I thank You for the inflow of the Spirit
    Through Jesus Christ, our Lord Amen

November 2

A Thought

Compassion is an outgoing caring that has no power aspect to it. It is the radiation of loving concern for another, because the love of Christ 'constraineth us'.

A Prayer
Lord grant me the power to see ourselves as others see us
And so to learn from my effect on others
  that I reflect You
    Amen

November 3

A Thought

The phone rang in the middle of the night. It was a friend of a friend who wanted to commit suicide.

'I should never have been born,' she said, 'I didn't want to be born and no one wanted me to be born.'

I felt I had to go to her, to show her she was wanted now. So I went.

I think it helped. At least she is – years later – alive and happy.

A Prayer
Make me a channel of your peace
Where there is despair, let me bring hope
Where there is sadness, let me bring joy
Where there is hatred, let me bring love

Amen
(based on words by Sebastian Temple)

November 4

A Thought

Colonel Alida Bosshardt, who, as I have said, worked in the Red Light area of Amsterdam for 27 years, speaks of the broken contact between God and man and the need for reconciliation. So evangelism involves the ministry of the Word, the offering of the Gospel to all wherever they are and however far off the awful country to which they have gone, 'with the purpose of bringing them to the faith.'

A Prayer
Here am I, Lord
  send me
    with words of comfort
      gestures of love
        thoughts of strength
          hearts of hope
  to all Your people

                        Amen

November 5

A Thought

Alida Bosshardt's view of pastoral care is that it is 'the work of the Shepherd bringing comfort and guidance through the Word in order to build up faith and deepen spiritual lives.' The purpose of both evangelism and pastoral care is 'the preaching of the Word that is not of ourselves but is of God; the Word of forgiveness, renewal and hope, revealed in and through Christ.' It is 'Christ for the world, the world for Christ.'

A Prayer
Turning my eyes upon You, O God
  and looking on the face of Christ
May I find the cares of the world
  pass into oblivion

                        Amen

November 6

A Thought

Suffering was something Christ knew, because it was part of being human in the free world God had made. Illness is something that should not be. If there is dis-ease present within us, something has gone wrong that need not have done so.

It is God's will that we do all we can to relieve dis-ease.

A Prayer
In days of uncertainty
  be sure and steadfast, O Lord
In days of unknowing
  touch the deadened intuition
  heal shattered faith
In days of rejection
  renew Your acceptance of us, as we are
In days of resurrection
  give us joy and peace

                    Amen

November 7

A Thought

Healing ministry is not an extra-ordinary ministry within the church, but *normal* ministry. Jesus used two phrases, not one, in His commands to His disciples. They were 'Preach the Gospel' *and* 'Heal the sick.' Both are mandatory.

A Prayer
Grant me insight, O Lord
  into myself
  into others and
  into the ways of the Spirit
Then may I find the doorway
  to growth in grace
  and the likeness of Jesus Christ

                    Amen

November 8

A Thought
The more I think about the relationship between the physical, the mental, the emotional and the spiritual, the more fascinating becomes the concept of health, and the more important our constant consideration of the nature of healing. Dis-ease in any part does seem related to dis-ease of the whole.

A Prayer
Graciously deal with me O God
   when I fall short of Your hopes
   when I compromise Your standards
   when I disobey Your will
   when I fail in charity
Through your grace, may I begin again
   and feel hope-full

                    Amen

November 9

A Thought
Martin Israel has a profound understanding of the inner healing processes and of the healing of the memories. Accepting as he does, 'the corruption that lies deeply within us' he writes in *Smouldering Fire*: 'The work of the Spirit in regenerating the unconscious mind by redeeming deeply hidden paradoxes is the basis of the healing process.' Integration is, I say again, through the Spirit.

A Prayer
The good that I would,
   I do not, O Lord
The evil that I would not,
   That I do

Who shall deliver me from this death,
  the law in my members that when
  I would do good, evil is present within me?
I thank God
  'Through Jesus Christ, our Lord'

                                    Amen

November 10

A Thought

So many of our assessments of people are based either on limited knowledge or lack of real knowledge that it is not surprising that we often err in our judgements. We cannot know everything about everyone, but at least the realisation of that limitation will make us cautious in the evaluations to which we commit ourselves.

A Prayer
Make me care-full in judgement
  truth-full in criticism
  grace-full in relationship
  wonder-full in encounter
Never let me lose the sense of the holy
  in You and Your creation

                                    Amen

November 11

A Thought

The fifth of six steps suggested for those who 'seek to love creatively' is this: 'Whatever your profession or occupation cultivate the listening ear, the penetrating mind, the observant eye, the loving heart, the gentle voice and the humble spirit.'

A Prayer
O God,
    strengthen within me the will to serve
    create within me the heart to love
    renew within me the desire to give
    seal within me the gifts of grace

                              Amen

November 12

A Thought

  'I saw you coming down the western road,

  My heart laid down its load'

  That Chinese couplet of the fourth century BC sums up the wonder
of the loving heart.

A Prayer
Let peace begin with me, O Lord
  For only so, can I be a peace-maker
Let truth begin with me, O Lord
  For only so, can I forward truth in the world
Let Love begin with me, O Lord
  For only so, can I add to the love
    the world needs

                              Amen

November 13

A Thought

The concept of the Logos is used by John in his Gospel to proclaim
two of the great purposes of the Word, who is Christ. The first is that
He is *the Revealer of God* and the second that He is *the Saviour of
Men*. In both capacities, He is God's *healing* Word.

A Prayer
Draw me nearer
  nearer
    nearer, O Lord
So that I receive from You
  grace
    power
      peace
Making me a more effective disciple

Amen

November 14

A Thought

The human perspective and the divine perspective are so different. What seems to be a serious sin in the understanding of men – and this often depends largely on the mores of the moment or the current cultural context – may look very different to the One who sees not in part, but in whole, not through a glass darkly, but with the clarity and charity of the divine understanding.

It is this attribute of God that makes so truly for healing. We may hide our faults and failings from our friends and fear the disillusionment that surely must follow their discovery, but God is a different proposition. He is (as St John reminds us, 2:25) 'well aware of what human nature is like.' He knows *before* we ask, confess or plead. It is out of His understanding of us in our totality that healing begins.

A Prayer
Glow, with Your 'Fire Divine', O God
  in my heart
make it radiant
  warm
    loving

enfolding others in its 'warm embrace'
as You have enfolded us
in the embrace of Your love

Amen

November 15

A Thought

God sees our worst before others – or even we ourselves – do. Is that a counsel of despair? It is the reverse. It is the word of hope we need, the word of comfort for which we yearn. Healing begins, is continued and ends in the divine awareness, understanding, forgiveness, acceptance and sanctification of us. It is there life begins anew.

A Prayer
Begin Your miracle of grace in me, O Lord
 through Jesus Christ
Continue the growth of grace in me, O Lord
 through Jesus Christ
Finish Your new creation of me, O Lord
through Jesus Christ
And I will bless You, the author and finisher of my faith

Amen

November 16

A Thought

In the pastoral care of people, it is no use pretending they are where they ought to be or that they are what they are meant to be, when the reality is quite different. The only hope for ministry begins with the acceptance that they are what they are, 'warts and all'. Then, and only then, will the road to improvement open up.

A Prayer
Accept me, Lord
  Just as I am
    confused
    compromising
    capricious
Make me, Lord
  what You want me to be
And this I leave in Your hands

                    Amen

November 17

A Thought

The minister, showing us his Weimar church, said a lot about its architecture, its stained glass, its organ. He did not say his wife was dying.

'The show must go on' is a great tradition that is not confined to the stage. There is often much personal suffering, unseen, behind pastoral ministry.

A Prayer
Let my face be bright
  though my heart be heavy
Let my love be real
  though love has been lost
Let my care be rich
  though care I have not
Let me give of friendship
  even when I stand alone
The grace to do this I ask
  through Jesus Christ, our Lord

                    Amen

November 18

A Thought

The Paraclete is the healer in three ways: first, the Spirit is the *Comforter* in the root meaning of that word. The Spirit gives strength. The Spirit is, secondly, the *Consoler* for we need consolation. Thirdly, the Spirit of our *Advocate*. He speaks on our behalf.

'The Spirit itself makes the intercession for us.' That is good news, for that is a healing process indeed.

A Prayer
I rejoice in the Good News
   God is Love!
   Christ is risen!
   The Spirit has come!
   Forgiveness is free!
I bless You for this News
   for it leads to life

Amen

November 19

A Thought

'Deep speaks to deep' says the Psalmist. It *is* true – psychologically and spiritually. So beware if you listen to or hear part of such a conversation, for you may be on another level and you may misunderstand.

A Prayer
Give me integrity, O Lord
   and let me not then worry about criticism
Give me conviction, O Lord
   and help me triumph over hurt
Give me peace, O Lord,
   so shall I be unmoved by hostility

Amen

November 20

A Thought

It is God's will that (as Paul says in 1 Timothy 2:4) 'all men shall be saved and come to a knowledge of the truth.' In the end, all will return to the God who made them if they can, like the Prodigal Son, 'come to themselves'.

So God waits in patience for His recalcitrant people, not in anger or irritation, but with the Divine longing that lies eternally in His heart. We are called to reflect that patience.

A Prayer
O God, I love You
not because 'I hope for heaven thereby'
but because You first loved me
Seal that relationship
through grace amid faith
Then may 1 live in relationship to You
all the days of my life

                              Amen

November 21

A Thought

Of all the Old Testament passages dealing with 'pastoral' work, that which comes from Ezekiel (34:11, 15-16, *NEB*), is surely as I noted earlier, the most moving: 'I myself will tend my flock, I myself pen them in their fold, says the Lord God... I will search for the lost, recover the straggler, bandage the hurt, strengthen the sick, leave the healthy and strong to play, and give them their proper food.'

A Prayer
Faced by the grief and pain of mankind,
Grant me Your understanding, O Lord
so that I may help constructively
* minister creatively*

encourage graciously
So may my ministry be seen as guided and upheld by You

Amen

November 22

A Thought
The Master helps and heals today through the power of the Holy Spirit He promised. If this is not reality, then the Gospel is a mockery. It is reality and so the ministry 'in His name' must go on to demonstrate not only His power in the past but the promise of the 'greater works' that will bear witness to His power today. 'His touch has not lost its ancient power.'

A Prayer
Grant me Your peace, O God
* as I look back over this day*
and repent of its wrongs
as 1 sleep this night
as I face tomorrow
and all it brings for me to do
Let me wake refreshed and ready
to serve You more and more

Amen

November 23

A Thought
Sensitivity is not sentimentality. It is an attitude that sometimes has to express itself in strength. It was the sensitivity of Christ to the need to recognise human freedom and responsibility that allowed the rich young ruler to leave whereas sentimentality or sympathy of a softer kind might have wanted to try to ease his way into the Kingdom. Love had the sensitivity to let the young man go.

A Prayer
I triumph still
  If You abide with me
So let Your presence be with me
  Always

                                        Amen

November 24

A Thought
'To gain insight into oneself, to come to oneself, to learn to know oneself' says Alida Bosshardt, 'all this happens when Christianity functions properly. Efficient social work functions similarly. Christianity has an extra dimension however. There is a greater Power at work. It is a Power that can totally change a person and lead to conversion'.

A Prayer
Touch my heart Lord, and let there be
  compassion
    tenderness
      gentleness
        love
in what I offer to those in need

                                        Amen

November 25

A Thought
Joy, an inner quality, rather than an outward emotional or physical expression, is an attribute of God Himself, so human joy is a reflection of Divine joy just as love is a reflection of the Divine love.
'Rejoice always.
Again, I say, rejoice'

A Prayer
May I in heavenly love abide
  and feel secure
May I in heavenly joy abide
  and feel glad
May I in heavenly grace abide
  and feel at peace

                    Amen

November 26

A Thought
Christian joy is not an ethereal quality associated only with the soul,
nor is it merely pleasurable gratification associated with the body. It is
a product of grace and faith that is related to our wholeness, and this
can be felt only when two yearnings are satisfied – our deeply felt
spiritual needs and our legitimate delight in the senses, when
dedicated to the glory of God.

A Prayer
I see You, O God
  in the beauty of nature
I sense You, O God
  in the mystery of revelation
I feel You, O God
  in the 'love I receive'
I offer You, O God
  the love I can give

                    Amen

November 27

A Thought
One of the most healing words in the Bible is the word 'redemption'.
It whispers of sin forgiven. It speaks of new opportunity. It sings of
freedom and it shouts of hope.

A Prayer
Let me not proclaim my failings, Lord
  You know them all
    and whisper forgiveness
Let me rather proclaim Your love, O Lord
  I know it for
    I have felt it often
May the value of my failings be
  the door they open
    to help others towards forgiveness, too

                    Amen

November 28

A Thought

'Redemption... sings of freedom' – the freedom implicit in the changed new life. It deals not only with the past through the renewal of the present. It looks to the future. It opens inner doors, releases creativity, offers true liberty. It must therefore shout 'hope'!

A Prayer
I am saved by hope, O Lord
  The sense of Your constancy
  The knowledge of Your final victory
  The assurance of Your continuing presence
  lighten and gladden my future
May I walk in Your light
  and rejoice in Your love

                    Amen

November 29

A Thought

Redemption is concerned with the healing of the memories, both conscious and unconscious – beyond our conscious awareness. It is

only as the Holy Spirit first probes, then penetrates the unconscious areas of our lives that 'conversion', or fundamental change occurs.
It is in these deepest, inner areas that the Holy Spirit must move in redemptive activity and renewing grace.

A Prayer
Remember me, O Lord
  in my weaknesses but also
    in my strengths
  in my failings but also
    in my successes
Grant me the honesty to see
  where 1 have been wrong
And the humility to acknowledge
  where 1 have had success
And through both
  lead me toward true righteousness

                    Amen

November 30

A Thought
The miracle of redemption is that the worst we have or are becomes the most potentially creative part of ourselves that we can offer. Selfish aggressiveness redeemed can become dedicated energy devoted to the blessing of mankind. Lust redeemed can be the compassion of love and the love of compassion that ministers to need. Anxiety understood can become a quality of peace-fulness that 'passes understanding' and passes its tranquillity to others.
Redemption is the activity of God in Christ through the Spirit and in that context it is a wholly healing process,

A Prayer
May my whole being reflect
  the grace of our Lord Jesus Christ
  the love of God and
  the fellowship of the Holy Spirit, the Comforter

        Through Jesus Christ, our Lord Amen

DECEMBER

God with us

December 1

A Thought

When Dr John White, one of the most famous ministers ever at the Barony Church in Glasgow, was asked the secret of his spiritual resources, he answered simply: 'I met a Man.'

Grace is mediated in many ways – a distant encounter with a voice, a close encounter of a fleeting kind with someone on the path, a loving relationship with a like mind or heart, an intimate and a profound meeting of souls across a decade, the life-long companionship of another. There is someone somewhere who has blessed your way.

I met a man...

I met a woman...

I met...

A Prayer

Thank You, O God

  for those with whom I have found rapport

  for those in whom I have sensed Your presence

  for those through whom I have gained in insight

  from those whom I have loved and who have loved me

Thanks be to You, O God, for meetings

  with those who do us good

Through Jesus Christ, our Lord

                    Amen

December 2

A Thought

'Take with you words,' said Hosea (see August 16). Words can be an instrument of peace, an orchestration of joy, a symphony of the sounds of salvation. Through words, Christ the Word is made known.

A Prayer
I wait on You, O God
  to renew my strength
    to run and not be weary
      to walk and not faint
May I be renewed in my waiting

Amen

December 3

A Thought

To enter the human condition on the stage of history, at the time He did and in the place He did, was to face the problems of expectation. For Israel was earnestly looking for the Messiah who would deliver the Rome-dominated nation from its oppressors, the One who would 'redeem Israel'.

Jesus was crucified because He did not come up to expectations.

A Prayer
  May the spirit of reconciliation
be in me, O God
So that I may reconcile and bless wherever I go
So may I truly be
  a minister of reconciliation

Amen

December 4

A Thought

When I met that great Japanese Christian, Toyohiko Kagawa, *The Saint in the Slums*, the concept of humility, as I had always envisaged it, became incarnate. His influence (as my recording it some 20 or more years later shows) has remained. I met a man of grace, graciousness and gracefulness.

True humility is, in truth, a mark of the man in Christ.

A Prayer
As I journey on, dear Lord
　be a companion on my way
　be a courier for my way
　be a welcoming host at the end of the way
　So may I feel I have never been alone on the journey

Amen

December 5

A Thought

Humility is a mark of the Christian. It will always 'increase' us rather than decrease us, if we can find the secret of it. It is when we set out to be boastful and conceited that we lose spiritual stature for Love 'vaunteth not itself, is not puffed up.' It is only when we clothe ourselves in the garments of humility that we truly grow.

A Prayer
Give me tolerance, O Lord
　so that I
　　bear with the unbearable
　　have patience with the trying
　　have understanding for the provoking
　　And when I come near to my wits' end
Grant me yet more grace

Amen

December 6

A Thought

Humility is not a denial of one's worth. It is a recognition of it.

A Prayer
Grant me, O God
　the grace of humility
In, all my labours

prevent me from concern with prestige, position and
popularity
Make my satisfaction, and my pleasure,
   the doing of Your will

Amen

December 7

A Thought

We are. Paul tells us, 'letters from Christ' (2 Corinthians 3:3). We have therefore a pastoral purpose to fulfil on paper *and* in person.

A Prayer
Help me to feel the loneliness of others
   and understand their yearning for friends
Help me to sense the anxiety of others
   and respond to it with sensitivity
Help me to be aware of the fears of others
   and offer the love that casts out fear
Help me to know the pain, of others
   and so minister relevantly to it

Amen

December 8

A Thought

As salt permeating the earth has its secret effect (Matthew 5:13), so must disciples influence the life of the world. So with light. As lights shining in the world, so must disciples 'shine'. For where there is salt or light, things will begin to happen. New life will begin to grow.
'I am the light of the world' (John 9:5), 'Let your light so shine before men that they may see your good works and glorify your Father which is in heaven' (Matthew 5:16).

   Light brings warmth: warmth creates life.

A Prayer
In a world often cold
  help me to offer warmth, O God
In a world often hard
  help me to ease the path of others
In a world often gloomy
  help me to generate joy
In a world often sad
  help me to offer comfort

                Amen

December 9

A Thought

We are not prevented, if we are determined to do it, from going to 'the far country' as the Prodigal Son did. The Father will wait for us.

The rich young ruler was free to say 'No' and go away perhaps later to ruminate and possibly to return.

It is not the Divine way to overwhelm personality against one's will, but it is of the essence of the Divine will to long and to wait, in order, ultimately, to receive.

'There is joy in heaven over one sinner that repenteth.'

A Prayer
Let heaven's arches ring
  and the angels sing
    when I return, penitent
      to Your love
To be dead, then alive
  lost and then found
    is an experience of blessing
For which I give thanks

                Amen

December 10

A Thought

Justification (or spiritual turning-point) and sanctification (or spiritual growth) are not possible without the realities we cannot prove, but by which we live and on which we base all... that God was incarnate in Jesus Christ, that the risen Christ promised the living, active energy and presence of the Holy Spirit.

These are the fundamentals of our faith and we cannot treat them as if they were not true,

Love divine exists.

New life is offered.

A Prayer
Let there be light
  along my way
Let there be love around me
  on the way
Let there be life
  as the way unfolds

                              Amen

December 11

A Thought

The Christian doctrine of forgiveness is of primary importance for it is the most therapeutic of all doctrines. An understanding of the meaning of forgiveness will give a balance to life that is crucial, and provide a perspective on life that is sound.

Life should not be gloomy with guilt, but glad because there is forgiveness. It is real! Believe it!

A Prayer
Make my life, O Lord
  a melody of grace
  a dance of joy
  a song of hope
  a vesper of peace

                    Amen

December 12

A Thought

Holy worldliness involves 'involvement' *and* 'distance'. 'Worldliness' is the involvement. 'Holiness' implies distance. It is not the Christian's function to opt out of the world. As with Christ Himself, his only possible place is within it. It is the Christian's responsibility to realise the call to holiness and accept the true apartness involved. The recovery of apartness and, in that sense, holiness, must be a discipline for all who seek to grow in grace. It is easier to be 'worldly' than to be 'holy'.

A Prayer
When tension fills my body
  grant me, O God, Your peace
Let peace, like a river, flow through me
  bringing relaxation, rest and regeneration
So may I be renewed in body and soul

                    Amen

December 13

A Thought

It is the claim of the Christian faith that the insight into life which came in Jesus Christ and comes through the power of the Spirit provides a true perspective on life and leads to balance and wholeness. The attainment of that true perspective must be the aim and prayer of the sanctified soul.

A Prayer
Make me to move quickly
  when obedience demands, O Lord
Help me to walk slowly
  when growth requires it
Let me take up enthusiastically
  new projects of grace
Keep me consistent
  in all I undertake
For You are constant and never change

  Amen

December 14

A Thought

The words of Jesus to the two disciples who walked the Emmaus road were very strong! 'O fools,' He said, 'and slow of heart to believe all that the prophets have spoken! Ought not Christ to have suffered these things?' To which the answer must be: 'Yes, of course' for only thus, it seems, could He 'enter His glory'.

A Prayer
Lord, forgive me if my anger is unrighteous
  my envy is uncontrollable
  my jealousy is real
  my irritation is inexcusable
Give me rather the gentle graces
  through the power of Your Spirit

  Amen

December 15

A Thought

There is plenty of room for divine eccentricity and enthusiastic individualism in the service of the kingdom (otherwise how can we ever be 'fools for Christ's sake'?) but beneath and around the life motivated by the Spirit, there is a balance, an order, a harmony and a wholeness that speaks of His presence.

A Prayer
You *are my shepherd, O Lord*
  I shall want nothing
You restore my soul
You lead me in right paths
Filled with Your love
I shall fear no evil
For You are with me
  Always

                                   Amen

December 16

A Thought
Caution converted becomes commitment, Thomas' declaration of belief on the receipt of the proof he requested, becomes outstanding conviction to be remembered, for all time, by his cry: 'My Lord and my God!' (John 20:28). It is a cry from the same level to the same level as was Mary Magdalene's: 'My Master' (John 20:16). Once the truth is revealed, you can and must throw caution to the winds!

A Prayer
O Lord, make me bold in
  all I think
  in all I plan,
  in all I do
So that I represent the faith
  I claim to hold
    with courage

                                   Amen

December 17

A Thought

Grace reaches down into the very depths of the human struggle, which is a war in the soul between good and evil; a war between all that is on the side of good and is therefore uplifting, strengthening, inspiring, purifying and invigorating and all that belongs to evil – that which lowers, degrades, defiles, make less, reduces in spiritual stature. All these latter things are grace-less. 'Love never does the grace-less thing' (1 Corinthians 13:5, William Barclay).

A Prayer
If I forget You, O Lord
  forget not me
If I fail You, O Lord
  leave me not comfortless
If I lose You, O Lord
  lose not me
If my love is weak, O Lord
  still love me

                    Amen

December 18

A Thought

Goodness like so much in the spiritual area becomes less attainable the more we *try* to achieve it, for goodness is a product, not an aim. It is the result of the Spirit's work within us. It is most visible to others when we ourselves cannot see it. It has most effect on the world when we are not aware that we are proclaiming it.

A Prayer
When I look on the crowded world in my prayers
Help me O God, not to be overwhelmed by its problems for
I cannot solve them all

Nor can I have significant influence on them
But enable me to see that
What I can give I must give
What I can influence, I must try to influence

                              Amen

December 19

A Thought

I once interviewed someone who had worked for 10 years in animal welfare. I asked her why. 'It was to pay my debt to animals,' she said. 'Debt?' I said.

'Yes,' she replied. 'I was beaten and battered by my parents as a young child, so I should have grown up unloving and unloved. But I had a dog, who loved me and whom I loved. That dog prevented me from losing the capacity to know and show love.'

A Prayer
Oh Master, grant that I may never seek
  so much to be consoled as to console
  to be understood as to understand
  to be loved as to love
    with all my soul

                        Amen

                    (based on words by Sebastian Temple)

December 20

A Thought

You would expect that those who earnestly discussed questions of theology relating to the crucified and risen Christ on the road to Emmaus, would be aware of his presence. But they didn't recognise him. Theology by itself does not open eyes to the real presence of the Lord. So let us beware of making academic discussion about Christ a substitute for faith.

A Prayer
Lead me, Lord
  Lead me in Your righteousness
Make my way plain,
  And grant me safety

                        Amen

December 21

A Thought
So subtle and insinuating are the forces of so-called sophistication that, as with Pharaoh's ever-hardening heart, we fail to sense the diminution in our standards and find ourselves sharing in attitudes to life, death and people that fall short of our deeper desires and do not speak of our true selves.

A Prayer
Prevent, O Lord
  the hardening of my heart
  with its
    loss of pity
      lack of sensitivity
        lessening love
Draw me with the cords of love
  and so increase
    my compassion
      my understanding
        my responses
  that I move through life
  reflecting the example of my Lord

                        Amen

December 22

A Thought

'When the soul has purified himself' writes St Denis, a fifteenth-century mystic, 'when she burns with the fire of charity, when she shines by reason of her virtues, God takes His pleasure greatly in her. He holds her familiarly like a fair spouse, clasping her, caressing her, embracing her and communicating His blessings to her, abundantly.'

A Prayer
In widening circles, I bring to You, O Lord
  the family
    the community
      the nation
        the world
          and the church, militant and triumphant
Hold them all in Your hands, I pray

                Amen

December 23

A Thought

Stars that have been followed with eagerness and enthusiasm have failed to lead to salvation, The belief that, first, education, then science, then psychology would provide the answers to all man's needs, lies crushed and broken.

  The false pursuits go on, but the Christian remedy remains,

  'There's none but Christ can satisfy.'

A Prayer
Into Your hands, O Lord
  I commit
  those who are ill
  those mentally troubled
  those nervously upset
  those anxious about tomorrow

se distressed about yesterday
nt each of them Your peace

Amen

December 24

A Thought
Christ has no hands but our hands
    to do His work today
Christ has no feet but our feet
    to lead men in His way
Christ has no lips but our lips
    to tell men that He died
Christ has no help but our help
    to bring them to His side

A Prayer
Use me, O Lord
    as You will
        when...
            where...
                how...
Grant only that I shall be
    obedient to 'the heavenly vision'
My promise I renew this holy Eve

Amen

December 25

A Thought
Follow the star, and find through it, like wise men of old, that you find your Lord. Find, in the holy Mary, a richness that enriches your whole life. Ponder the extra-ordinary self-giving of Joseph whose deeply spiritual intuition played such a part in making it possible for the holy child of Bethlehem to be 'ours today'.

A Prayer
O Holy Child of Bethlehem
  Descend to us, we pray
Cast out our sin and enter in
  Be born in us today
O come to us
  Abide with us
    Our Lord
      Immanuel
        God with us

Amen

(Phillips Brooks)

December 26

A Thought
Jürgen Moltmann, the German theologian, says that living in hope 'is an experiment'. He goes on: 'Hoping is a risky matter, it can bring disappointment and surprise developments. To live in hope is a mark of the Christian.'

We need a theology of hope today – and to take the risks involved.

A Prayer
It is never night
  if You are near, O Lord
It is never dark
  if Your light shines, O Lord
It is never bleak
  if Your warmth enfolds, O Lord

Amen

December 27

A Thought
It is hard to live and think and act as if 'the things that are seen are

temporal while the things that are not seen are eternal' (2 Corinthians 4:18). This, in worldly terms, is the opposite of truth and an invitation to foolishness. The physical is, of course, the 'real' to the world. The senses apprehend reality. To make the spiritual into reality is to fly in face of 'the facts', to court disaster.

Yet to do just that is the instruction on the Christian's 'map'. His is a map of life determined by that perspective. Because of it, he will see the whole of life, its meaning, its pain, its joy and its happenings in a different way.

A Prayer
I need You every hour
  O gracious Lord
    The pressures I face are heavy
    The problems I meet are grievous
    The solutions I seek are elusive
    The peace I need is gone
Grant me Your presence
  and Your peace, I pray

                              Amen

December 28

A Thought
There are, in life, the things which we cannot change – like age, physical limitation and similar hindrances with which we have to live. In such circumstances, we 'learn therewith to be content' as Paul reminds us. But the real limitations we accept must not lead us to forget that what we can change, we should change, especially if it is limiting or unworthy.

Let us keep alive the true spirit of the rebel within us!

A Prayer
The weight of the world's needs weighs heavily on me, O God
  I see that starving child
    and I cry within
  I hear the voice of the displaced person
    and from the security of my home, I worry
  I read of war and violence, constantly
    and I feel the pain of those who suffer through it
Lord, give me always
  an understanding heart
  a compassionate mind and
  a loving soul
Where any of Your children are in need

              Amen

December 29

A Thought
You may, in the eventide of life, say with Simeon that you can go on your journey in peace because your eyes have seen salvation. In the fullness of life you may join the crowds who spread their garments in the way of the Lord of life.

There is no fixed route to salvation and the health of the soul... though so many try to confine the Spirit by insisting that there is. What matters is that *we* find the way that leads to life.

A Prayer
May I give my heart to
  sympathy with the suffering, O Lord
May I give my mind to
  changing all that makes for suffering
May I give my strength to
  aiding the afflicted and helping the hurt

              Amen

December 30

A Thought
Ben Travers, the 93-year old playwright, wrote his own epitaph. It is:
'This is where the real fun begins.'

A Prayer
May hope spring eternal within me, O Lord, so that
   I never give up anyone as hope-less
   I never lose enthusiasm
   I never fail to be stimulated by the future
Thus, saved by hope, may I find life ever new

Amen

December 31

A Thought
'Do you see yonder shining Light?' asked Evangelist of Christian in
Pilgrim's Progress. 'I think I do' Christian said. 'Then,' said
Evangelist, 'keep that light in Your eye.'

A Prayer
Day by Day
Dear Lord of Thee
Three things J pray
   To see Thee more clearly
   To love Thee more dearly and
   To follow Thee more nearly
      Day by Day
May I make this prayer my own
   Each day of the new year
And serve You as You deserve
   A day at a time

Amen

(The prayer referred to is attributed to St Richard of Chichester)